"The Self-Aware Leader provides breakthrough ideas to grow the talent needed to achieve critical business goals. Author Dan Gallagher reveals the playbook utilized by Comcast to teach middle managers the keys to reinvention and professional self-awareness. His practical approach, perfectly geared toward today's generation of learners, will help you accelerate the development of high potentials destined for the executive suite. And, you'll be inspired toward a bit of personal reinvention yourself!"

Tacy M. Byham, PhD
VP Executive Development
DDI

"Look no further for a professional development book that shares pragmatic prose coupled with emotional intelligence-filled insights about a very necessary leadership trait—know thyself! *The Self-Aware Leader* will assist the reader in gaining wisdom to lead their team and organization with more courage, more empathy, and more clarity."

Kevin Carroll
Author of *Rules of the Red Rubber Ball, What's Your Red Rubber Ball?,*
The Red Rubber Ball at Work, and the Katalyst blog

"The Self-Aware Leader will take you on a thought-provoking journey, helping you pragmatically look in the mirror and assess your professional and emotional self-awareness. This book is filled with practical advice and examples that directly translate into actions each of us can take that will make a difference. This is the ideal companion if you have a desire to become a more effective leader and are willing to self-reflect and change."

Suzanne Keenan
Chief Information Officer
Wawa

"Drawing on a number of examples from Ben Franklin to Ice Cube, this book provides a fresh, contemporary look at the key role self-awareness plays in management success. Through compelling anecdotes drawn from years of Dan's experience in molding future corporate leaders, it offers fresh, practical advice to managers and provides the blueprint around which many management development programs should be constructed."

Dr. Roch Parayre
Senior Partner, Decision Strategies International and
Teaching Fellow of Executive Education, the Wharton School

The Self-Aware Leader

Daniel P. Gallagher
Joseph Costal

Alexandria, Virginia

ASTD Press is an internationally renowned source of insightful and practical information on workplace learning and performance topics, including training basics, evaluation and return on investment, instructional systems development, elearning, leadership, and career development. Visit us at www.astd.org/astdpress.

Ordering information: Books published by ASTD Press can be purchased by visiting our website at store.astd.org or by calling 800.628.2783 or 703.683.8100.

Library of Congress Control Number: 2012934021
ISBN-10: 1-56286-812-8
ISBN-13: 978-1-56286-812-3

ASTD Press Editorial Staff:
Director: Anthony Allen
Senior Manager, Production & Editorial: Glenn Saltzman
Project Manager, Content Acquisition: Kristin Husak
Associate Editor: Heidi Smith
Design and Production: Abella Publishing Services, LLC
Cover Design: Ana Ilieva Foreman
Printed by Data Reproductions, Auburn Hills, MI, hwww.datarepro.com

Dedication

This book is dedicated to our beautiful brides, Suzanne and Shannon. We married sisters and we married up. It brought us together and has given us such rich lives—as husbands, fathers, and friends. Suzanne and Shannon, we love you, we cherish you, and we thank you—every day!

Many other people supported us through the three-year process of writing this book. For that we are truly grateful. While we cannot list all of them, below are a select few we are especially grateful to. Thank you!

- Martha Soehren, David Cohen, Brian Mossor, and Tom Nathan from Comcast for your tremendous support.

- The hundreds of Comcast Fundamentals of Leadership graduates for opening yourselves up to reinvention and giving this triangle a story to tell.

- Justin Brusino, Kristin Husak, and Heidi Smith from ASTD for a truly wonderful partnership.

- Mark Marrow for your brilliant approach to providing editorial input.

- Ron Dufresne, PhD, and Lucy Ford, PhD, for your expertise and collaboration on the research.

- Michael Brown, Nancy Routh, Sean Holleran, and Rebecca Byrne from City Year for your idealism and inspiration.

- Pat McGrory, Jeff Taylor, Connie Bernard, Jim Andrews, and Marcia O'Connor for your friendship and feedback.

- Joe Laipple and Barbara Cowan for assigning the first deadline.

- Bill Novak and Jessica Papin for your votes of confidence.

- For Jack, Luke, Quinn, Reece, Charlie, Finn, Tallulah, and Henry—thank you for the joy you bring to our lives every day.

Table of Contents

FOREWORD

At the November 1863 dedication of the Gettysburg National Cemetery, where tens of thousands of fallen Civil War soldiers had been buried, Secretary of State Edward Everett, then considered by many to be the era's greatest American orator, spoke for two full hours. Next to speak was President Abraham Lincoln. His speech, which would become known as The Gettysburg Address—"the words that remade America" according to historian Gary Wills—was all of 272 words long. Lincoln spoke with characteristic vision and humility. He called for a "new birth of freedom," emphasizing the Declaration of Independence and its call for equality as the founding ideal of our nation for which so many had just given their lives.

Only a self-aware leader could summon, on this somber and important occasion, the wisdom and perspective necessary to be as brief and modest as Lincoln—and yet to evoke a cause and ideal so much larger than self—and, as a result, to be as persuasive and history-making.

This same self-awareness led Lincoln to incorporate his political opponents into his cabinet, forming what historian Doris Kearns Goodwin called his "team of rivals." Rather than telling everyone around him what to do, Lincoln listened to his rivals, often replying with stories that would at once disarm and signal the way forward.

Lincoln knew that he cut an unusual figure for a president. His gangly physical appearance and country lawyer demeanor had a unique effect on people, and not one that necessarily commanded immediate respect or reverence among Washington's most powerful. Those who judged Lincoln too quickly based on his appearance or folksy approach to governing undoubtedly did so at their own peril. He was easily underestimated, especially by elites.

Few could argue that Lincoln did not embrace the concepts of self-awareness and reinvention that Dan Gallagher describes so compellingly in this book. Lincoln is perhaps the most self-aware leader this country has ever had. He is also the one leader who not only saved the union, but also most reinvented the United States—as a nation that strove truly to live up to its founding declaration that "all men are created equal." And although Lincoln's death provided little time for America to witness the full measure of his magis—the wonderful Latin term for generosity of spirit that Dan Gallagher speaks of in this book—through his leadership he made us a more self-aware country. Lincoln's magis echoes across our land today, like a beacon of grace, and a challenge for our time and all times.

In the pages that follow, Dan Gallagher speaks powerfully and persuasively about how the self-aware leader "reinvents self," "reinvents others," and "reinvents the business," leveraging this reinvention for success whether in a for-profit or nonprofit organization.

As CEO and co-founder of a national education-focused service organization, City Year, I have been at the helm of an organizational reinvention during the past several years.

We started City Year in Boston with a simple yet powerful idea: young people have the idealism and energy to change the world. We set out to establish a demonstration site to prove that young people in national service can be an instrument for real change in society. We deployed a corps of idealistic young people to serve full-time for a year, helping nonprofits carry out a variety of community projects—including working in schools, building community gardens, and assisting seniors—while earning a small stipend and a post-service scholarship.

We developed a strong culture, based on values including empathy, diversity, inclusivity, and altruism, and focused on developing the leadership qualities and skills of the young people who serve in our corps. President George H.W. Bush provided our first federal support, and in 1993, when President Clinton founded AmeriCorps, he credited City Year—and a visit he made during his campaign to City Year headquarters—with inspiring the federal service program. Today all of our corps members are AmeriCorps members. Over the years, we expanded, adding new City Year sites in communities around the country.

And then nearly 20 years after our founding, we realized it was time for a reinvention. While we had succeeded at training future leaders and conducting quality service projects, we did not believe that we had cracked the formula for achieving an aggregate national impact against a problem that society critically needed to be solved. After an intense period of organizational reflection—and a deeper review of what was most pressing and relevant to the needs of the nation, we decided to focus our work exclusively on addressing the nation's high school dropout crisis.

Every 26 seconds another student gives up on school in America, resulting in more than one million American high school students dropping out every year. In our knowledge-based economy, dropping out of high school is a fast track to an underclass. Dropouts are three times more likely to be unemployed and eight times more likely to be in prison than high school graduates. Studies have found that, if left unabated, the 10 million young people who drop out in the next decade will cost society $3 trillion in social costs. With barely 50 percent of the nation's young minorities graduating high school, access to a quality education (as U.S. Secretary of Education Arne Duncan has said) is the civil rights issue of our time.

Today, City Year unites young people of all backgrounds for a year of full-time service to keep students in school and on track to graduate. At City Year's 23 locations across the United States and at two international affiliates, more than 2,000 highly-trained corps members serve full time in schools as tutors, mentors, and role models. By focusing on attendance, behavior, and course performance—indicators that research shows can identify which students are at risk of dropping out—City Year AmeriCorps members provide evidence-based, one-on-one, and whole-school interventions that help students and schools succeed.

Our transformation was not easy, but it has been deeply rewarding. We are seeing exciting results in the high-need schools where we serve.

Self-awareness has been—and continues to be—critical to this work. Our corps member leadership development model emphasizes reflection and self-knowledge, as well as other leadership skills. At the staff level, our senior team regularly pauses to reflect thoughtfully on our strengths and challenges, building a culture of honest assessment and a hunger for constant improvement throughout the organization.

Self-awareness has also been important in my own career as a CEO. There was a time, for example, when I did all my work at a whiteboard, drilling down on the issue of the day with a marker in hand. As the organization has grown and my role has evolved, however, I have needed to shift my focus and hone different leadership skills—including learning to get out of the way and to get into a supportive role for the enormous talent around me.

* * *

Dan Gallagher is a wise man at a wise company, Comcast. And this is a wise book. At City Year we have had the privilege of having Dan's personal pro bono investment in the development of our talent at every step of the way for over a decade. I can personally attest to the power of his ideas in action.

The importance of self-awareness is often overlooked, but Dan Gallagher sheds light on this crucial leadership quality in a way that will have real relevance to leaders across sectors and at all career stages.

I am sure that as you read on, you will see yourself in this book's pages. The examples are poignant, the lessons are resonant, and the takeaways are clear. The ideas in this book are not just back-of-the-napkin notions. The book's principles are aligned with research and its messages are versatile with a wide array of applications. As you read ahead, you will find both a new mental framework on leadership and a functional, practical plan for putting it into practice.

Reinvent self, reinvent others, reinvent the business. It is a great model and a great message.

—*Michael Brown, CEO and co-founder of City Year, Inc.*

INTRODUCTION

If we are all creatures of habit, and history repeats itself, then the world is basically a series of patterns. People who can anticipate these patterns will have greater success than those who cannot. This is not about making bold predictions like Nostradamus, Vegas Vic, or even Al Roker. This is about stepping outside of what is happening and being aware of how to use that insight to be more effective.

You can be stuck in traffic in your car wondering why you are not moving, or you could be viewing the traffic jam from a helicopter analyzing the same 4-mile gridlock. Both experiences allow you to see the same thing—but the different views teach you different things.

One of my most memorable assignments in college was to visit the world-renowned Barnes Foundation art museum. We were told to spend an afternoon wandering the gallery and observing. But we were not to observe the paintings themselves—we were to observe the people. After recovering from a few strange looks, I began to understand the point of the assignment. Our professor's contention was that learning comes from both doing and from watching what others do.

Few film directors read the reviews of their films. But almost all of them attend premieres. There, they can watch the audience. Hear applause. Measure gasps, laughs, or screams. Only then does the true effect of their work and its quality become apparent. In this way, my professor was right. Observe the observer, and a greater truth shines through.

The same can be said of holidays. You lumber through decorating, cooking, and shopping. You focus on accomplishing these small, but vital tasks. You are driven by lists. You charge through the chronology with little regard to the meaning behind the moments. Until…you take the time to observe. It's only when we pause to take in what is really happening that the true spirit of the season emerges.

Leadership works in the exact same way. Some of my greatest lessons in leadership have come not from studying the concept itself, but by observing those who practice it. These days, as an executive who develops leaders at a Fortune 100 company, my work is still informed by this lesson. Successful leaders are great observers. They are keen and vigilant. They still need to execute to be excellent, but they know that self-awareness guides them in how to effectively execute.

This book is designed to sharpen the self-awareness of middle managers. These leaders often find themselves in the most unenviable of leadership roles: buffering between employees and upper management. Being a middle manager takes patience and loyalty. Yet, most middle managers are overly focused on simply just getting things done.

The leadership model presented in this book applies to young up-and-comers looking for a launching pad and to journeymen veterans looking to ward off stagnancy. The model has been tested on hundreds of middle managers just like you and validated in empirical research that specifically highlights what leadership self-awareness drives career growth.

Two important keys to leadership success are to: (1) reinvent to remain relevant and (2) make moves that are proactive, not reactive. Middle managers need to be reminded that they are the masters of their own destiny. Your position in the middle affords you greater reach and access. You communicate with more players than anyone else at the table, because you are, after all, in the middle of all the action. People look to you before making their own moves and you need to do the same. Self-aware leaders grow on their own, predicting and shaping change by observing the patterns of others to influence their own patterns of behavior.

The Proactive Work of Middle Managers

The *Self-Aware Leader* is different from many other leadership books because it aims to inspire *proactive and calculated action* rather than *reaction* to change. It is the first to fully integrate the idea of reinvention, servant leadership, and business transformation into a single framework. This strategy can be the first step of your own leadership reinvention, or for the leaders in your organization. Another key difference is that this book forces its readers to accept three sometimes hard, cold realities about succeeding in organizations:

- Everything has a shelf life.
- Middle managers are really caught between "a rock and a hard place."
- With corporate conservatism on the rise, leadership is tough.

Everything we do has a shelf life—including our leadership styles and basic work skills. In today's competitive landscape, no individual or organization can ignore the basic fact that all good ideas and management styles have an expiration date. Everyone accepts that businesses must change quarter to quarter to optimize results, yet those same individuals often use a much more relaxed timeline to affect any changes in their own career approaches. Waiting for the world, or your team, or your organization, or your boss to push for or lead change does nothing to help your career and will more likely put it in jeopardy.

The second reality is that today's middle managers are in a tough position, stuck between trying to figure out how to merge personal and professional fulfillment while being tethered to their BlackBerries 24/7. On one hand, there might be some merit to keeping a low profile and just working hard. While this is a safe strategy, it is not exactly leadership. On the other hand, you are more likely to be rewarded by being visible, vocal, and creative. These visible leaders stick out their necks for the good of progress and engage in debate. They recognize that moving forward means breaking from the past. Yet, this cavalier, lead-the-pack attitude can be dangerous, even disastrous. Middle managers who act as change agents sometimes advance ideas that call into question or undermine past decisions of senior management. Not a great way to make friends in upper management.

A third reality of the corporate world is that corporate conservatism is on the rise. Fully mature initiatives are still seeing cutbacks. New ideas are deflated simply because the dollars are not there to even try. In addition, most companies now ask their employees to do more with less. As a result, employees feel burned out from overwork and as a result of past layoffs and reorganizations. The consequence of these realities is a bitter, complacent workforce. Clearly middle managers with 20 years left in their careers are not ready to coast.

Enter the Self-Aware Leader

Current business realities and research for this book have convinced me that self-awareness is key to the ultimate success of middle managers. In fact, this book argues that self-awareness should be the absolute foundation of leadership programs. Why is it important to be self-aware? What does self-awareness look and feel like? In answering these questions, readers will learn how to leverage self-awareness to reinvent themselves as leaders.

The one thing this book won't offer you is a way to statistically assess your individual self-awareness; plenty of other books and instruments can help you with that. However, you will learn important lessons about the aspects of your career you should be aware of and which characteristics drive leadership outcomes like promotions, better projects, and professional satisfaction. Don't worry. You won't be overloaded with complex statistical analysis, but at the same time there is more here than a good idea on a cocktail napkin.

Perhaps the most important lesson of this book is that it teaches you how to leverage self-awareness in specific ways that drive professional reinvention. The guiding light for your reinvention journey is an interdependent model with three elements: the reinvention of self, the reinvention of others, and the reinvention of business.

Reinventing Leadership

- **Reinvent Self** teaches you how to grow new skills and leverage these on a larger platform on which imaginative ideas become substantive solutions.

- **Reinvent Others** teaches you how to use inclusion and collaboration as a tool for increasing the productivity of others, and therefore yourself.

- **Reinvent the Business** creates a lens for you to look at your organization, projects, and decisions in terms of profits, products, services, and people.

In the end, readers will walk away from this book with two key takeaways:

- a new mental framework on leadership
- a functional, practical plan for putting it into practice.

You will learn what levers to pull and when to pull them to create upward mobility. You can use the system for yourself, your team, or your organization, whether your work is for a profit or nonprofit entity.

Description of Chapters: Section 1

The book is divided into three sections. Section 1 focuses on the foundation of the book and defines the model. It explains "the what" as validated by my research and explains how I use this model to train leaders in a Fortune 100 company.

- **Chapter 1 — The Self-Aware Leader's Advantage:** Self-awareness is positioned as the center of this book and the foundation of leadership. The chapter defines self-awareness based on the trends identified in research. The impact self-awareness has on business and individual productivity is also highlighted with examples. Finally, readers learn how self-awareness changes how others see them.

- **Chapter 2 — A Proven Path to Becoming a Self-Aware Leader:** This chapter introduces a model that calls for leaders to proactively reinvent themselves. The key to being able to know when and how to do this is self-awareness. Leaders learn about three types of reinvention: self, others, and business. The three are interdependent, and therefore must be part of any leader's portfolio for consistent career progress.

- **Chapter 3 — The Four Pillars of Reinvention:** Leaders learn of four pillars that connect self-awareness to reinvention. The pillars are: (1) an above-average network and support system, (2) a proficiency in critical and systems thinking, (3) a savvy perspective of the political landscape and (4) a courageous drive for magis (defined as doing more for the good of others). Each pillar is described with key principles, supporting items, and related examples.

Description of Chapters: Section 2

Section 2 connects key leadership principles and demonstrates how self-awareness drives professional reinvention. It shows how each principle can be applied to individuals within an organization. Most chapters also include an opportunity for the reader to reflect on what they have read, answer a few questions, and think about applying the principle. The application could either be individual or could create more sweeping cultural change in an entire organization.

- **Chapter 4 — Professional Authenticity:** This chapter begins a series that addresses the core principles driving self-awareness. Professional authenticity calls for leaders to explore and embrace their own individuality and recognize how discounting it can decrease productivity and increase professional stress. Practical examples and self-assessment questions further define this term.

- **Chapter 5 — Profitable Imagination:** This chapter will encourage readers to tap into the potential of their imagination by using it to grow their organizations. Profitable imagination challenges readers to be progressive and productive with how they think about innovation—in what they are doing and how they do it. Dr. Joe Laipple's science of "working backward" is introduced to teach readers how to connect their imagination to what their customers need most.

- **Chapter 6 — Generosity Quotient™:** Once leaders have ideas in place, they face a significant decision. Do they keep their ideas and contacts to create more value for themselves or do they share the wealth? Readers will learn the secret: leaders create their value by inclusion and empowerment. This chapter defines Generosity Quotient™ and presents different ways to put it into action: champion, catalyst, coach, and confidant.

- **Chapter 7 — Think Like a General Manager:** General Managers (GMs) lead in all directions and across all functions. They see how one aspect of an operation influences others. This chapter teaches readers to look at projects, jobs, and decisions as a GM would. It uses a very simple approach that is further described through the use of a "four buckets" analogy which illustrates how the principle of "cross-functional love" knocks down silos in both mind and practice.

- **Chapter 8 — Feed a Family Versus Solve World Hunger:** This chapter focuses on the art of pinpointing as a critical factor in defining success. Too many individuals and organizations attempt to bite off more than they can chew. The result is partial success on aggressive, unrealistic goals rather than full success on practical goals. The reader learns how to use judgment, science, and precision to clarify priorities.

- **Chapter 9 — Who You Know Versus Who Knows You:** This chapter provides a targeted approach for growing the reader's network and provides reasons why. Readers are asked to assess the value of their network. Does it help them become more self-aware? Are people intentionally included in their support system? Readers are taught how to proactively manage their network to prepare for collaboration and promotions.

- **Chapter 10 — Connect the Dots and Spur Innovation:** Connecting the dots is about linking two seemingly unrelated things. It's about using your profitable imagination and ability to think like a GM in a way that spurs innovation. This chapter explains how analyzing patterns and using maps will provide you with strong data to help you plan your next reinvention.

- **Conclusion —** The conclusion integrates all the book's leadership principles. This will provide guideposts for the reader's action plan. Emphasis is also placed on pacing your reinvention.

Description of Chapters: Appendix

The appendix expands on the individual and organizational focus by introducing additional details on self-awareness and reinvention for those readers charged with building leadership development for their organization. It is intended to bring together the specific points and techniques in one place to make the job of translating the self-aware leader into deployable training programs. Additional support information can be found at www.gallagherleadership.com.

- **Appendix A — Implementing as the Training Department:** This section describes how to design curriculum and facilitate leadership development programs that drive behavioral changes within individuals and is directed to learning and development professionals.

In Summary

In the end, the lessons of this book are clear, practical, and proven. By *reinventing self*, we ensure relevance by proactively upgrading skills to reflect the leadership traits of tomorrow. By *reinventing others*, we ensure leadership is more than of just self—that people are being led. By *reinventing the business*, we use diversity of thought to propel growth. Self-awareness will drive reinvention. What will drive you?

Section One

The Foundation

Chapter One

THE SELF-AWARE
LEADER'S ADVANTAGE

"To be nobody but yourself in a world that is doing its
best to make you just like everybody else means to fight the
greatest battle there is to fight and to never stop fighting."

—e. e. cummings, American poet, essayist, author

Comcast Corporation is one of the world's leading media, entertainment, and communications companies. It employs more than 107,000 employees worldwide and reported an income in 2010 of nearly $36 billion. It has reinvented the business by launching a number of new products in the last 10 years, some of which today individually generate more than $1 billion in revenue. It has also multiplied its workforce by over five times since 2002. As you might expect, Comcast spends a lot of time training leaders to drive their growth.

The self-awareness leadership principles in this book are the same ones that underpin a Comcast high potential middle manager training program I designed in 2003. Since that time I have complemented my years of internal practice with both internal and external research. I knew the story had strong themes and as I spoke with colleagues at other for-profit and nonprofit organizations, I realized the themes were not unique to Comcast. This was the persona of the modern day manager.

The research-based findings along with long-standing experience make a convincing case that organizations that ignore the importance of self-awareness do so at their own peril. Throughout this book several of the most significant research points will be highlighted. Make no mistake, self-aware leaders are more effective and their impact is felt in dramatic ways throughout the organization.

A Disclaimer

Although it's tempting to make promises, I am not going to do it. No magical powers or painless way of reinventing yourself or your organization's leaders into charismatic, self-aware individuals is offered in the following pages. No book can make such a promise. What the book does offer, however, is a clearly defined path toward building a more self-aware and effective leadership pool. You can use this book and the systematic approach it offers as a basis for your own self-awareness development or as a template to help other leaders. It's all up to you. The book develops your concept of self-awareness; you develop you!

Whatever your intended purpose, this book has the potential to significantly change how you approach your job and your life. But remember, such dramatic results are not free nor are they easy. The journey is challenging and in the end it's up to you to find the courage and internal resources to complete the trip.

The Middle Management Profile

A middle manager is characterized as someone who is supervising frontline leaders. In most cases they have direct reports who manage other direct reports. For example a call center manager/director has a call center supervisor who has 10 call center agents on her team. The key here is not to get caught up in job titles but rather to look at the scope of responsibility. Middle managers are not responsible for doing all the work themselves. They are responsible for getting others to do the work. They guide, coach, direct, and hold people accountable. In the majority of cases they are only responsible for one functional area, but are seeking to be promoted into roles that manage multiple functional areas, or have work that significantly affects other functions more blatantly.

Now, the beauty of this audience versus a more junior audience is that they have been around the block a few times. They've been kicked in the shins. They know what they're good at and have aspirations to grow. Middle management, as compared to the next level up, has not fully made their minds up on the type of leader they want to become. They are still open and willing to work on their development.

The principles of self-awareness in this book are particularly successful with this specific population because they need this help getting to the next level. Middle managers are motivated to observe more about themselves. Now one could say that all employees need more self-awareness to get to the next level, and while that is true, this book truly focuses on what aspects of self-awareness these middle managers need in order to drive their success.

The Study of Self-Awareness

Every year Comcast identifies 45 high potential leaders to participate in a year-long development program. These leaders have demonstrated exceptional proficiency at the middle manager level and have been earmarked as the next generation of directors. The premise of the leadership model in this book was actually built for this program. We start with a 360-degree assessment. And every year, we see the same trends for the high potential leaders currently working in mid-level management. The results are included on the next page. The aggregate scores are really interesting because the strongest behaviors (the highs) and the lowest behaviors (the lows) provide a deeper understanding of these high potential leaders. The data presents the best of their strengths and their greatest needs for future success.

Self-Awareness From 360-Degree Feedback

One of the best ways to assess self-awareness is through a 360-degree feedback tool. The respondent asks their boss, peers, direct reports, and others for feedback on the same questions evaluating their leadership. The anonymous feedback offers candid, data-driven answers from all directions and allows the receiver to take a holistic view of how others perceive them. It is worth repeating, however, that it measures perception, not actual performance.

A 360-degree feedback tool teaches us that a leader's proficiency, while overall consistent, can often vary greatly when applied to different populations. In other words, a leader's strengths vary depending on the population. For example, a given leader may be great at listening to upper management, and the data will show this. Yet, that same leader may "score" lower on listening to her direct reports. Awareness of this variance of skills as they are applied to different populations is extremely valuable. It reveals that the weakness is in application and not in a total skill gap.

The data exposes answers to a leader's difficult questions. This given leader, for example, may have found success at getting support for new initiatives from executives, but she may have struggled with implementation with the team. Most people just look at something more general like listening skills and consider themselves either good or bad at it.

The next page lists 10 behaviors most highly rated for the participants in three different "fundamentals of leadership" classes. The data is a compilation of responses from direct reports, peers, and immediate supervisors of the participants in this program. The trends in the data show consistency with this population in their strengths—a consistency that was repeated more than just the three years indicated here. If you look across the years at the behaviors listed in bold, you will see these groups of high potential middle managers are workhorses. They put in the hours and get the work done. Sounds like people you'd want working for you, right? The only problem is they have direct reports and when they, as a leader, do all the work, your business is overpaying to get the work done. Yet when you think about the reinvention model (business, others, self), these leaders are not focusing on others in this list of highs.

AGGREGATE 360 HIGHS = Workhorses		
2007	**2008**	**2009**
1 Readily puts in extra time and effort	Knows the job	Readily puts in extra time and effort
2 Protects confidential information	Gets the job done	Protects confidential information
3 Knows the job	Readily puts in extra time and effort	Gets the job done
4 Gets the job done	Protects confidential information	Sets high personal standards of performance
5 Sets high personal standards of performance	Produces high quality work	Knows the job
6 Learns new information quickly	Displays high energy level	Produces high quality work
7 Produces high quality work	Learns new Information quickly	Puts top priority on getting results
8 Develops effective working relationships with higher management	Sets high standards of performance	Accomplishes a great deal
9 Understands the organization's mission, vision, strengths, and weaknesses	Conveys a sense of urgency when appropriate	Understands the organization's mission, vision, strengths, and weaknesses
10 Accomplishes a great deal	Accomplishes a great deal	Learns new information quickly

The good news is that this group is open to hearing what they have to do to get to the next level. When you show these leaders this 360-degree feedback, they clearly see the impact of how others perceive them. Their awareness only increases when you share with them their aggregate lows.

Similarly, the 10 lowest behaviors listed on page 7 specifically define the aggregate development opportunities for these same three classes. The most prominent trend is that these leaders tend to exclude others in the process of being workhorses. Again, this trend is represented by three years of data in this chart, but the trend has been prominent for much longer. Here's the selling point: If you are a middle manager today, you probably manage 10–20 people in your entire team. If you want to grow to the next level, that number could double. If you do all the work of your 10 reports today by controlling everything, how in the world will you do the work of 30 tomorrow by yourself?

> Self-awareness is knowing yourself, your own personality, and your leadership style. Self-awareness comes from what you know about yourself as well as what you learn about yourself from others. You must know your strengths and weaknesses to be able to identify opportunities for growth."
>
> —The United States Army Website

But as any good researcher knows, you cannot just stop at the data and consider yourself done. You must be able to build and tell the story that explains the data—that makes it relevant. There are three main stories that come from this data.

Most middle managers fit in the classic leadership model as one of two types of leaders: task-oriented or people-oriented. The people tendency is seen in things like influence, communication, and relationship-building skills. The tasks tendency is more focused on achieving results and managing execution. This is a trend that is very obvious at the middle manager level, but when the same assessment is distributed to upper management, the trend disappears. Why? A leader can get away with this lack of balance in managing a single function or team. When you progress to managing a more complex team or even multiple teams, however, executive-level leaders must find balance. They cannot afford to depend only on themselves. Not only would this create a time management nightmare, but also, no one wants to work for this type of micromanager. If you aspire to be any title with a "C" at the beginning, resist the temptation to view people as simply a means to an end. No one ever developed loyalty for a boss who saw them as vessels for carrying out tasks. Avoiding this transactional approach to the work world may be harder than it seems. Recognize people, especially colleagues and direct reports, as fully dimensional human beings. Acknowledge that who they

AGGREGATE 360 LOWS = Control Freaks		
2007	**2008**	**2009**
1 Delegates assignments to the lowest appropriate level	Delegates enough of own work to others	Delegates enough of own work to others
2 Delegates enough of own work to others	Delegates assignments to the lowest appropriate level	Delegates assignments to the lowest appropriate level
3 Adapts approach to motivate each individual	Adapts approach to motivate each individual	Takes people's preferences into account when making decisions
4 Accurately defines strengths and development needs in others	Accurately defines strengths and development needs in others	**Compromises to build give and take relationships with others**
5 **Challenges others to make tough choices**	**Knows when to supervise and coach people and knows when to leave them alone**	**Knows when to supervise and coach people and knows when to leave them alone**
6 Readily commands attention and respect in groups	Knows the strengths and weaknesses of competitors	Knows which battles are worth fighting
7 **Knows when to supervise and coach people and knows when to leave them alone**	**Challenges others to make tough choices**	Expresses disagreement tactfully and sensitively
8 Expresses disagreement tactfully and sensitively	**Compromises to build give and take relationships with others**	**Analyzes problems from different points of view**
9 Involves others in shaping plans and decisions that affect them	**Analyzes problems from different points of view**	Anticipates the positions and reactions of others appropriately
10 Deals constructively with own failures and mistakes	Confronts problems early before they get out of hand	**Challenges others to make tough choices**

are is so much more important than what they are worth to you or your organization. The beauty is, the more you care, the more they'll care. The more you value them, the more they'll want to be valuable to you and your organization.

Most middle managers are better at getting things done themselves than they are at getting things done through others. They believe the old, misguided adage, "if you want something done right, you should do it yourself." This thinking has failed them. Instead, they should be developing the self-awareness to realize that very often, "something is only done *right* if done by your team." Many of these managers were promoted because they are strong individual contributors, but they stay in "doer mode" even after their promotions. Their direct reports would respond better if they would spend at least as much time empowering as doing it themselves. At Comcast we ask our high potentials about 154 behaviors. For six consecutive years, three of the top five behaviors in most need of improvement included the word *delegation* in the behavior label. These managers actually lacked the ability to execute on the definition of management: to get work done through others. The organization is then overpaying to get the work done. This may work in the short term, when a leader is managing one function, but in an upper management role in which the leader has responsibility for multiple teams, it will burn them out personally and set them up for failure professionally.

Most middle managers hear the voices in their heads before they hear the voices of their employees. These voices assist high potentials in thinking a plan through while other people in the room are just starting to grasp the particulars. In other words, their trains arrive in "I have a great idea" town before other people's trains of thought have even left the stations. The challenge is that these great ideas often affect their ability to listen. They need to learn one simple truth; beneath every great idea is a well-timed introduction. Full speed ahead is not always the best way to see your vision implemented. While processing ability and predictive nature are signs of great intelligence, sometimes, they can be as much of a curse as a blessing. Uncle Ben told Peter Parker: "With great power comes great responsibility." Well, a leader's intelligence is only as powerful as the responsibility he uses to guide it. Everyone wants leaders who are mentally capable. Yet, my research has shown that those who process information faster than others can think or communicate it, are bound for frustration and tension. It can strain relationships that may otherwise lead to valuable professional partnerships. Some know the answers and want to drive forward, but they don't always recognize the impact their drive has on others.

When looking to hire someone, a self-aware leader asks, "Tell me about a time when you used your voice to make a point when really you should have used someone else's." This sometimes throws people, but I like having the opportunity to explain what I mean to prospective employees. First, it gets them thinking about their *voice* to begin with. You see, writers are very aware of *voice*. It's the vehicle for which they make their style unique. Some writers—think Cormac McCarthy or even Charles Dickens—have such a unique voice that even the most casual fan could pick their prose out of a lineup. The same should be true of leaders. A self-aware leader is aware of her voice. She works on it. She reflects on her style and promotes her distinction from other leaders. A leader's voice is optimal when it provides a note of tension relief in a room. Good leaders know they have mastered their voice if others perk up, smile, or speak around them. In other words, their voices inspire other voices.

Yet, too much of anything is not good for you. No matter how well-crafted a leader's voice, there are particular instances when it can frustrate and stymie others. We tend to see this as the other person's problem. The problem is actually that the leader's voice is eclipsing the others around her. No one likes that, and plainly, a true leader guides and cultivates other voices around her. Once your voice is too big for your reports to hear themselves, you have failed them as a leader. To remedy or prevent this, the leader must hone her intelligence within the context of social intelligence.

Candidates interviewing for management roles are quick to talk about the ways or the times they "saved the day." A much better gauge of leadership would be to speak about the times you promoted someone else's voice into a position to save the day. The self-aware leader balances social intelligence into her cerebral or functional intelligences to create a grace and understanding of those around her. Then she knows she cannot always be the first person to put the idea on the table.

Is It Them or Me?

Ever share a room with a group of colleagues or acquaintances when suddenly someone's stomach emits a massive growl? Even the most politely aloof individual will look around the room. Undoubtedly, someone in this situation will usually, just to break the ice or ease the tension, pat their stomach and blame a late start or heavy traffic. He draws the attention to himself. He wonders aloud what everyone wonders silently, "could it be me?" It's funny and comforting because it reveals people's basic insecurity. Normally, the person who diverts in this way is one of two things:

- confident enough that the growl did not come from him
- self-aware enough to own the growl when it did not belong to him.

This may seem like a silly example, but this type of action is a vital and often little-used indicator of self-awareness. The higher a leader climbs, the more important it is for her to be aware of the sights, sounds, and smells within a room of colleagues. Every room you walk into is going to smell of something. Success? Failure? Inertia? Fear? Before pointing fingers, the self-aware leader recognizes how she could be contributing to the stench of problems or to the sweet smell of success. Dr. Edward W. Deming, an American statistician who is recognized by Japan as one of their greatest thought leaders in the area of manufacturing quality, always preached that management is the source of 85 percent of the problems, as they own the systems. This logic, when applied to self-awareness, calls on leaders to (a) recognize they are in that 85 percent and (b) own the system that is contributing to the problem. This exercise in observation influences the voice the leader should take to be most effective.

Two Sides of the Same Coin

There are actually two forms of self-awareness. Gaining self-awareness in either area is equally challenging, but both are necessary for driving leadership success.

The first is **professional self-awareness**.

It calls for individuals to know their strengths and weaknesses. When great leaders say that they surround themselves with people who are smarter than they are, it's not fully true. Leaders know what kinds of specific smarts they need to hire: the kind they don't have themselves. This aspect of self-awareness is interesting.

Let's use Steve as an example for this. Steve was an individual contributor who aspired to middle management. He had the experience in years but there were some skills that held him back. His manager asked him to meet with a senior stakeholder to get some feedback. The two had worked together on and off, but had never really had any significant conversations about careers. The short story on Steve was that he could crank out highly complex work, but very few folks really got excited about working with him. When Steve asked for feedback, he was really asking for help to grow his self-awareness. Here's how the conversation went:

> COACH: *"You're a very strong individual contributor, Steve. You are tremendously smart and talented and have a solid work ethic. But before I answer your request for feedback, let me ask you a question, OK?"*
>
> STEVE: *"Sure, that's fine. I'm more than happy to answer a question. I really want to dig into this."*
>
> COACH: *"What is your career goal, Steve? Would you rather be a very expensive consultant who works for yourself…a specialist? Or would you rather be running a shop at a major corporation of 10–20 people who are doing this type of work as part of your team?"*

Steve paused and seemed perplexed. He wasn't sure where the feedback was going. He was wondering why the coach was framing questions rather than giving him specific feedback or better yet, prescriptive advice. But Steve's advice called for self-awareness. The answer was in the question itself. The coach was trying to open Steve's eyes by forcing him to answer it. He thought the coach was interested in his career goals, but the question was meant to expose his lack of self-awareness. The coach persisted amidst his wondering.

> COACH: *"Steve, here's the reason I ask. If your career goal is to run your own business as a high-end consultant, you are ready to go.*

You are brilliant, and you are also not very collaborative. I don't always feel that you are working to set others up for success—that you are thinking beyond the task at hand and toward the big picture. I'd hire you as a consultant on the spot. You are a genius at your specific job tasks. But I would not hire you on my team as you are today because I do not think you are as committed to putting in the time to bring significant contributions to the rest of my team or my clients."

Steve wanted to move up in our organization. If he aspired to be a consultant, he wouldn't have entertained the question. It was a catalyst for Steve's reinvention. Steve realized at that moment that he severely lacked self-awareness. Sure, this may have been the first time he had received such specific and deliberate feedback. But everyone deserves that level of feedback. After all, haven't you had good people in your life that helped you professionally with strong messages? They weren't always fun to deliver or receive, but they were valuable.

The second type of self-awareness is **emotional self-awareness**.

This one is tough. It is way more difficult than producing a list of another leader's strengths and weaknesses. This is your ability to hit curveballs and herd butterflies. Emotional self-awareness is about adaptability, altering behaviors, and being effective even in situations where you don't think you fit. It's about being calm when you are mad or being engaged when you are ready to move on to the next topic. Daniel Goleman was right when he included self-awareness as an ingredient of emotional intelligence, and he was even more right to list it first.

I remember early in my career being coached by a senior leader, Linda, who said, "Dan, you've been successful at just about everything you've done in your first six months here. What I'm waiting for is to see how you perform when you screw up." At first I was ticked. Really ticked. What kind of senior leader wishes negative experiences for someone who was working as hard as I was? It wasn't until about three years later when I was going through a major challenge in my career that I realized Linda's point. She had no desire of seeing me fail, she just knew from experience that not every six months of my career may come together as nicely as my first six with her. Anyone can look good on a sunny day. She wanted to see what I looked like in a hurricane.

Emotional self-awareness is experiential and situational. It recognizes that no two scenarios are the same, but history does repeat itself and therefore teaches all of us. It calls out the fact that not everyone is reading the same script as you are. Everyone has different motives and agendas. They see different paths to success for their projects and themselves. But most of all, emotional self-awareness recognizes that in order to be a strong leader you must thrive in ambiguity.

Emotional self-awareness can be difficult to identify. It's a challenging place to be because it's very ambiguous and abstract. Take Mary, the leader of a 300+ person team. She had been leading them for well over five years and people liked her. She was seen as a strong player and was very comfortable in her own skin. In fact, she could rattle off the list of strengths and weaknesses for her professional self-awareness without hesitation. But Mary's 360-degree feedback data showed something that her coach saw as an interesting opportunity to grow self awareness.

COACH: *"Mary, I know you are a leadership geek, like me, so before we dive in, I'd like to ask you a question. Does that work?"*

MARY: *"Sure, that works. I've taken these tools before so I have a hunch I know where you are going."*

COACH: *"Mary, do you consider yourself more of a CEO or a COO?"*

MARY: *"Huh?"*

COACH: *"When you think about how you spend your time, does it feel more like you are CEO of your group or COO?"*

MARY: *"I never thought of it that way. I'd have to say COO."*

COACH: *"And that's what your team would say. The odd thing is they want you to be CEO. You've been with them for more than five years. They know what you want and how you want it. And every time you continue to be COO, it comes across as a lack of trust in them to do their jobs."*

There are plenty of Marys out there who struggle in this area. She is troubled by finding the right balance between being CEO of her work and COO. The CEO role asks the leader to take on a visionary, inspirational role, staying focused on the future state. The COO role, however, dives much deeper into daily operations and regularly injects her two cents as to whether things are on track. In her role of leading 300 people, Mary is really asked to do both. Her leadership brand however, is stamped by those decisions in the moment to choose one over the other. The difference may be small on a regular Thursday afternoon meeting, but aggregate these differences over the course of a month and the trend speaks loudly. If Mary chooses the CEO role too much, the frontline may see Mary as a visionary but out of touch with reality. But, if Mary chooses the COO role too much, the frontline begins to question whether Mary really trusts them and their ability to execute. The key is being able to find an appropriate balance. And Mary must be able to read right to find an appropriate balance. Staying in tune with your self-awareness is an ongoing opportunity. Your world changes every day and that's what keeps it exciting.

What's the Advantage of Self-Awareness?

Self-awareness is proven to drive success of leaders in what they accomplish and how they are perceived by others. The key differentiator is knowing what to be self-aware of and then understanding how to respond. The table on the next page is composed of two columns. The left column identifies questions from opposing sides that are the common traps for self-awareness. These questions are traps with no obvious answer. Direction comes from asking yourself questions that will grow self-awareness. These questions are what push you into the observation mode before you act. As you read the questions, think about an example that you have witnessed firsthand, or even experienced firsthand. Odds are you have seen or felt them all. The advantage comes from knowing that these curveballs are coming, and intentionally slowing yourself down to ask the questions before jumping right into action.

Situation	Questions Self-Aware Leaders Ask Themselves
Should I listen to others? vs. Should I listen to myself?	• What is the group's body language telling me? Are there healthy debates happening or does that need to be instigated? • If I skipped a meeting or let someone else run a meeting, would the momentum carry at the same pace or in the same direction? • What would be the impact of my steamrolling this point? Will it help move the group forward or am I just on a power trip?
Do I go with the flow? vs. Do I push back?	• Why am I so obsessed with this point? Why isn't anyone else? Is the mission critical or am I just personally passionate about it? • Will not doing this severely damage my team's chances for success, or is it something that I want? Can I compromise? • Does the team have the same sense of urgency that I do? If not, what are they seeing, hearing, or sensing that I am not seeing?
Is this working? vs. Why isn't this working?	• Do different people view success in different terms? Has the definition of success been put in writing? Do all agree? • Is my success negatively affecting someone's work? Should I care about all groups equally? • Does the working team see progress the same as the leadership?

This shift in observing before acting is not something that happens overnight. This is something that takes practice, persistence, and patience. Done well, the advantage will create value for you as an individual, for your team, and for the organization. It will reinvent you to be more than you think you can be.

Chapter Summary

Self-awareness is a game changer. By recognizing what drives your own success and embracing the fact that this changes over time, leaders can proactively manage their leadership approach. The advantage is that not everyone takes the time to assess the leadership landscape as such. These leaders run the risk of becoming irrelevant.

There are two types of self-awareness:

- Professional self-awareness focuses on strengths and weaknesses.
- Emotional self-awareness focuses on your ability to thrive in ambiguity.

Leaders who strengthen each of the above can benefit by:

- balancing their focus on tasks versus people
- getting work done through others instead of themselves
- listening to others more than they listen to themselves.

Self-awareness is the foundation of reinvention. It serves as binoculars and as a compass. The binoculars allow you to see what's coming with ample time to navigate. The compass allows you to stay on track and feel confident about your changes in direction.

Chapter Two

A PROVEN PATH FOR BECOMING A SELF-AWARE LEADER

"What I am looking for is not out there; it is in me."
—Helen Keller, American activist, author

To stand the test of time, you must evolve. Anyone can react to a forced ideology shift, but great leaders predict, analyze, and change ahead of the trends. Most leaders have similar goals and most middle managers have their goals handed to them by upper management. What differentiates these leaders is how they achieve the goals. Call it creative execution. Leaders who recognize their need to listen, teach, and learn before they step on the gas will outperform those who don't. They are simply more self-aware.

Some of us are fortunate enough to work for companies that promote professional growth based solely on how quickly the business grows. But what happens if you work for a company that has extreme market saturation, no competition, or a product that will soon be out of style? Does that present a different challenge? When the playing field doesn't present any new challenges, professional stagnancy can creep in and permeate the work environment like mold. When the playing field doesn't propel change, it becomes the player's responsibility. This chapter provides the framework for that playing field. It will teach you how to reinvent and why that is important.

Ben Franklin's Influence

The idea for this reinvention model came about as I was managing *Fundamentals of Leadership*, an annual, high potential leadership development program for director-level management at Comcast. Each year, I would imagine a new theme and wrap the core leadership message around a tagline. The program was based in Philadelphia, so in 2006, the theme was rooted in celebrating Ben Franklin's 300th birthday. Just as Franklin had innovated, I was looking for leaders to look at themselves as products and reinvent. Through the program I challenged them to do something completely different without giving up who they are.

> The concept grew out of the notion that corporate leaders spend a great deal of time considering the reinvention of products and processes, but they put very few resources into reinventing themselves.

The program explored how each leader managed self, others, and the business. Each one of the three (self, others, and business) had a specific focus, yet they also all interacted as one model. Each leader had the ability to manage and control his own decisions. This program did not guarantee anyone a promotion as a result of participating, but it did guarantee they'd be challenged, stretched, and even pushed.

The Definition of Reinvention

The reinvention model is a holistic approach that calls for a lifelong commitment to upgrading oneself. It is based on the notion that leaders who invest in themselves and others will outproduce those who depend purely on *try* and *work harder*. True reinvention calls for daily experimentation. Thus, as you can imagine, this model will only work if adopted by someone willing to take initiative and risks. The model's tactics are logically structured. The definitions are digestible. The advice is practical. No super powers are required.

Reinvent Self teaches leaders to grow new individual skills and leverage them into a larger platform capable of turning imaginative ideas into substantive solutions. **Reinvent Others** teaches leaders to give time, energy, and focus on growing others as a methodology for demonstrating increased leadership stock. **Reinvent the Business** creates a lens for every leader to look at their organization, projects, and decisions in terms of four buckets: profits, products, services, and employees.

Reinventing Leadership

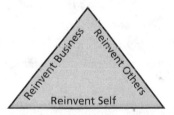

The only two requirements to implement this model are:

- Start with knowing yourself, but know that you don't need to start by reinventing yourself. This is where the foundation of self-awareness comes from and why **Reinvent Self** is the base of the model.

- Keep all three aspects of the model within your professional portfolio at all times. This means keeping each close enough that you can call upon it as needed.

There is no pressure to reinvent all three at the same time. Furthermore, how much emphasis you place on each will shift over time and define your evolving leadership brand.

Reinvent Self

You, like any product, must evolve to remain competitive. What worked for you five years ago may now be holding you back, or, at the very least, creating complacency. Your ideas, skills, and abilities have a shelf life. Many professionals ignore expiration dates. Instead, they cling to older, tried-and-true methods. Self-reinvention demands courage. The payoff, though, will leave you invigorated and re-energized.

Reinvent Self is about self-assessment. Fortune 100 companies are hiring young thoroughbreds that seem to walk out of college ready to rule the world. After only a few years, however, these same companies house a stable of dinosaurs. American corporations teem with professionals whose ideas and passions outdate their wing tip shoes. These lingering professionals are far more likely to refresh their wardrobes than their focus. They drag around the ideological equivalent of black parachute pants and a tan Members Only jacket from the 1980s. Just compare how many upgrades you have made this year to your wardrobe versus how many professional development exercises you have completed. See the point? The leaders who can self-reinvent are far more likely to add value to their organizations.

Even "original gangstas" agree. Consider Ice Cube—the original member of the hip-hop group, N.W.A, and a pioneer of gangsta rap. Ice Cube has always been one of music's most controversial figures. Rap is a youth-oriented medium, however, its stars are more aware of this than anyone. Facing the irrelevance that comes with being middle-aged, Ice Cube moved to films. Who could've guessed that someone responsible for some of the most violent and racially charged lyrics of the 1980s and 1990s would reinvent himself as one of the most financially viable family film stars of the 2000s? His 2005 film *Are We There Yet?* grossed 98 million dollars worldwide and spawned a popular franchise. Gangsta rapper Ice-T was best known for his controversial anti-police lyrics in the 1990s. Remember "Cop Killer?" Now, Ice-T can be found weekly on

CBS' Emmy-winning drama *Law and Order*, playing...you guessed it...a cop! Never underestimate the power of self-reinvention.

History illustrates that the greatest examples of self-reinvention come from those facing dire professional irrelevance. Consider Al Gore in 2000. Gore's flame had all but extinguished with his 2000 defeat, where he won the popular vote but not the White House. At the time of his concession, no one could've guessed the politician's looming reinvention. Gore the best-selling author? OK, that would've made sense. Gore the Oscar-winning documentarian? Um, seems like a bit of a stretch, but OK. Gore the Nobel Peace Prize winner? Holy Jimmy Carter! The butt of a thousand late-night punch lines is now the face of global warming. Gore went from professional irrelevance to resurgence faster than you can say "carbon dioxide." He has become quickly reinstated into the highest ranks of influence, simply because he had the courage to allow his passion for environmental issues to lead him toward reinvention.

So you're not Al Gore or Ice Cube. Not all feats of reinvention need to be all-consuming or high profile. In fact, this book highlights more than a handful of common folks who have put forward imagination, effort, and luck to reinvent to the highest degree. So don't worry if you don't have Warren Buffet's fortune, Oprah Winfrey's visibility, or Brad Pitt's looks. Your personal reinvention may not call for much more than a shift in how and where you expend your energy. Reinvention isn't about status and ambition as much as it is about passion and execution. Whether your focus is new or renewed, whether it is something you want to gain or something you don't want to lose, reinventing self stems from self-awareness of what you want to be.

Reinvent Others

Today's work environment calls for collaborators and developers. It is not possible to do it all yourself and expect to win. Those who are able to influence others will simply outpace and outproduce those who cannot. In addition, those who have the ability to influence multiple groups inside and outside their organizations are more valuable than those who live lives of one-track productivity. It plays off the old Vidal Sassoon adage, "If you don't look good, we don't look good."

Reinvent Others encourages leaders to give of themselves, not only at work, but also within the community. Selflessness is a way of life, not just a way of work. If IQ measures cognitive ability, and emotional intelligence (EQ) measures ability to perceive and manage emotions, then Generosity Quotient™ is one's ability to give. Generosity Quotient™ drives collaboration, consensus, and collective ownership. More attention will be dedicated to this new concept in chapter 6.

Opportunity greets us each morning with the sound of our alarm clocks. Henry David Thoreau felt that in the morning, the greatest happiness existed in anticipation of a day well lived. Nothing could be truer. Great teachers seize the opportunity to reinvent their students. Great doctors seize the opportunity to reinvent their patients. Great coaches seize the opportunity to reinvent their athletes. We use dozens of titles—coaches, mentors, teachers, fathers, sisters, friends—but at the end of the day, it's not the title, but the willingness to give of ourselves that inspires others.

Think about the best teacher or coach you've ever had. Ninety-nine percent of the time people can name their most memorable teacher or coach inside of three seconds. Why? We never forget those shoulders we have climbed upon to become who we are. Great teachers and coaches are more interested in the success of their students and athletes than in their own success. And we feel an insurmountable debt to this. Its value is not exclusive to the young. The spirit of teaching, coaching, and mentoring must become a more common part of professional life.

Whether you read this book as a business executive, college professor, nonprofit leader or lion tamer, the opportunity to inspire others awaits you, daily. In your office, there are colleagues struggling for a toehold in your company. Could their reinvention hinge on an encouraging word from you? In your industry, there are professionals mired in stagnancy and dwindling self-esteem. Could sharing a new idea or philosophy with them jump-start their own personal renaissance? Is there a spotlight shining on your success? Great, but true success only comes when you redirect some of that light on to those working hard around you.

Create an atmosphere around you in which others feel invigorated and energized, and yes, you too will feel more invigorated and energized. No one has ever been changed by singularly pursuing fame and fortune. To quote Chris McCandless, the great American hitchhiker also known as Alexander Supertramp, "Happiness is only real when shared." Choose encouragement over denouncement. Brag about others. Be someone who always points out what is possible instead of what is probable and watch the response from others.

> The definition of management is grounded in getting work done through others. The problem is that too often leaders are too busy or too insecure to share their trade with the "new kids on the block."

Managers fear losing the intellectual capital their organization values them for. They fear being eclipsed by a young hotshot. The funny thing is, this fear, or rather the paralyzing inaction it perpetuates, actually fosters professional irrelevance. You can do all the work yourself or you can orchestrate others doing the work. With the latter, your work is not about your output, it's about driving efficient and effective output by others. You don't have to always be the smartest person in the room. Sometimes leadership is just finding a way for the smart people to collaborate and innovate because they cannot do it by themselves. The point here is to embrace new professionals. Cultivate their growth, set them up for success, and watch your stock rise.

Further, this portion of the model could help you with the other two. In other words, one of the most powerful ways a leader can reinvent self is to share her intellectual capital and reinvent someone else to help grow the business. High potential employees are often coached to have their replacements fully-groomed to be successful in all aspects of their current jobs. The success of internal promotions will not only be based on how well an employee performs in her new role, but also how successful the employee's old team is without her. Look inside your organization at all the different generations. Will the grey-haired leaders in pinstripes listen to and debate with the nose-ring leaders wearing jeans? The definition of *normal* is being questioned and those who can relate to, engage with, and empower more people will be capable of achieving more progress.

Reinvent the Business

This one is simple. What sells today may not sell tomorrow. Others can quickly replicate your process. In fact, as you read this book, someone in a factory in China, a warehouse in India, or a garage in the middle of the United States is right now finding ways to replicate your business model at half the cost. Economic, social, and technological innovation forces organizations to perpetually master the art of reinventing their business—faster, better, and cheaper. It doesn't matter if you are for-profit or nonprofit, **Reinvent the Business** means business. If your organization isn't reinventing itself, it may find itself losing dollars and market share to the next great thing. Today's unstable global economy demands that we expect and respect the unexpected.

Reinvent the Business forces you to look at your organization in terms of healthy competition, even if it doesn't exist yet. A perfect example of reinventing the business is Starbucks. The linchpins of the 1990s gourmet coffee shop craze were quickly becoming viewed as overpriced by the mid-2000s. Starbucks seemed like its story was going to be rags to riches back to rags. In 2006, Starbucks was opening an average of six new stores a day. By 2009, Starbucks had posted an overall profits decrease of 70 percent, closed more than 600 stores, and laid off 7,000 employees. The thought of massive expansion in the midst of an economic collapse seemed destined to sour the caffeine empire. Luckily for Starbucks, they were already plotting reinvention.

Take for example their newly unveiled and highly publicized re-branding process. Starbucks changed its logo to remove the words *coffee* and even *Starbucks* from the image. The simple green, crowned, smiling woman will be the new face of the franchise moving forward. Many corporate critics have touted the move, hailing that it will allow Starbucks to grow outside of retail coffee, a seemingly necessary move given the continued collapse of their coffeehouse's profitability. What has been less publicized is that Starbucks' logo change is not the first step in reinvention, it's the last.

According to their 2010 Annual Report, Starbucks posted losses in their retail divisions. Yet, their fiscal successes came from the:

- promotion of the "Seattle's Best Coffee" brand (a cheaper gourmet coffee option)

- growth potential in China (a market Starbucks began focusing on in 2008)

- growth in their instant coffee and coffee appliances sectors (their instant brand touts "Starbucks quality for under $1 a cup")

- increased multimedia and Wi-Fi options in their retail outlets.

Starbucks is getting a lot of press for moving beyond just gourmet coffee into an international food player; so much so that many are ready to tout them as a complete "comeback story," but what seems like a redirection was a reinvention back when the Seattle coffee makers were king.

The *business* that needs to be reinvented can also be a nonprofit. In 2007, the IRS changed the rules for nonprofit tax deductions. Whereas under the old laws, a church just needed a ledger book and a discerning eye for donations over $250, the new law required more legitimate records. Doesn't seem like a big deal except that many places of worship depend on what they call "spur of the moment gifts." To combat what could've been a logistical nightmare and a major hit to their annual funds, churches began installing lobby ATMs. The move was less to promote donations and more to provide an easy solution to their paper trail problems with the IRS. Money directly withdrawn from an account leaves an automatic record perfect for bookkeeping. They also began accepting credit cards, another easy way to track deductions consistent with the new tax laws. To combat the natural tendency to judge (lest we be judged ourselves) such a money-oriented shift, the church got out in front of it in the press. According to a 2007 *TIME* article, pastors like to tell jokes about parishioners collecting frequent-flier points on the way to heaven. A recent *Dallas Morning News* poll found that 55 percent of 200 local churches accept credit and debit cards.

Why would churches innovate as such? Competition. Reinvented nonprofits realize that competition isn't just for corporate America anymore. Such accommodations beat back impending charter, private, and voucher school systems. Productive nonprofits now realize that they are competing with one another. They compete for customers the same way Pepsi competes with Coke.

Ben Franklin Meets Ed Cogan

Meet Ed Cogan: he is a normal guy. He has a normal family and home life. He works hard to maintain a normal career as a regional sales manager for a growing company. Ed knows he is good at his job, but like so many managers, he has no idea how good he could be. Until, that is, Ed learns how to reinvent.

Ed is handpicked to participate in Comcast's national high potential leadership program—the same reinvention program dedicated to Ben Franklin—one year later. Corporate will fly him to headquarters three times this year, where he will learn about leadership reinvention. Upon arriving, he listens with guarded skepticism. While he enjoys the two days of training, Ed wonders privately, "I need to grow sales. How is *that* going to help me?"

As part of the program, Ed and the other attendees are charged with completing a community service project. The project requires that Ed, in a finite amount of time, scopes a project with a community-based organization. Then he has to rally a team of volunteers and execute on the deliverable. Again, he is skeptical, but if he's going to have to do this, he may as well choose something he cares about. So, Ed designs a literacy project. It takes little effort, and it makes him feel good. "I must be a good leader after all," Ed thinks. But more importantly, the project awakens Ed's sense of purpose. He's no longer "just selling." He's also doing good for others, and that makes him feel good. Surprisingly, people begin seeing Ed differently. The project exposed them to a whole new side of him. He was able to display the type of passion, generosity, and vision that rarely shined through Ed's day-to-day management. Now, both Ed's sales reps and his management team respond to him more favorably. Ed suddenly puts stock in the upcoming leadership session.

Returning to headquarters, Ed learns that the literacy program was a discovery learning exercise designed to launch his own reinvention. Without even knowing it, Ed was conducting a personal renaissance, and the rewards were immediate. The generosity and service he displayed through the literacy project was leveraged into a leadership competency. Ed (and others) could see a noticeable difference, not to mention that his work benefited some local children. The second leadership workshop teaches Ed about problem solving, root cause analysis, and how to facilitate process improvement. This time, he returns to work charged with a new task: to solve a real business problem. Last time, Ed reinvented himself, and this time he will utilize his own reinvention to reinvent others and his business. The first project enhanced Ed's influence. Now he is charged with leveraging those skills. Ed will influence a business metric using structured problem solving. He begins exploring ways in which his team can increase sales. In the past, he did this by directing his team. This time, he begins by listening. The workshop has helped him mature as a leader. He now knows it is better to create value by valuing others. He now knows that he can best grow by allowing others to grow. Instead of directing, he facilitates. Instead of managing his team, he leads it.

Of course, Ed's team is more responsive than ever. When success comes, Ed highlights his team's work, remembering that his goal is to promote others, not himself. Ironically, his willingness to give credit to his team only further elevates Ed's status. Flying back for a third time, he is hooked on reinventing.

The final session focuses on the importance of perpetual reinvention. Ed realizes that he is only as good as his latest contribution. Continuing to reinvent his leadership brand will ensure Ed's success tomorrow. Rather than seeing this type of personal improvement as a chore, he views it as an energy source. It invigorates and focuses him. Whereas Ed once "just did" his job, now he is thinking about his career in a more global way. His job is just one aspect of his overall pursuit of an actualized leadership brand. By seeing his job as more than just his "work," but as one of the many leadership platforms available to him, Ed transforms into a more effective, more self-aware leader. It shines through him, his reports, his colleagues, his supervisors, his community, his family, and his friends. He focuses on innovation through perpetual reinvention.

Ed decides to turn his leadership project into a monthly event, and it quickly aggregates into a new way of conducting business. The same team of co-workers continues to volunteer with him. Four years later, Ed's monthly visits to Comer Hospital provide him the honor of introducing his management team to Michelle Obama, the hospital's then VP of community outreach. His process improvement projects on sales effectiveness have become the norm, and Ed's team glows with the knowledge that their work drove the projects. They now follow Ed's lead faithfully and brag to friends about the "time they met the First Lady."

Ed's success story is real. It's extraordinary, but it was achieved through very ordinary means. Ed transcended normal by making the fundamental and conscious decision to stop letting his career happen to him. He stopped letting leadership happen to him. He took control of the situation and built new plan and a new approach. In doing so, he positively affected all aspects of his life. Throughout this transformation, Ed remained the same humble person, except for one thing: he now had momentum and he understood what was generating it.

What Can Ed Teach Us About Reinvention?

At first, Ed didn't know just how much he didn't know. He was stuck but couldn't put his finger on why. He, like many of us, worked as hard as he could, and if he didn't meet his goals for the month, he'd simply work harder. What changed for Ed was self-awareness. He became more aware of his own need for professional satisfaction. Then he took that knowledge and compared it to what drives momentum in his work environment. Many leadership theorists hypothesize that all work can be boiled down into one of two things: people and tasks. But, knowledge of *what* work is doesn't help us learn *how* to get it done. The *how* is the prize in the Cracker Jacks. The *how* is what differentiates between good leaders and great leaders. The *how* is why some organizations perpetually grow and never coast. Ed's self-awareness grew in terms of the *how,* not the *what.*

So what do Ed Cogan, Ice Cube, and Starbucks have in common? They all saw the need to evolve before others did. On the surface, this sounds easy, but in reality, so few people do it well. How do you prepare yourself to reinvent? As indicated in the last chapter, the foresight comes from self-awareness. This foresight becomes a competitive advantage. Reinvention is not simply change. Change alone is not enough. Reinvention is change that adds value. In a time when everything from paper towels to paper bags is being called "new and improved," why not slap a big yellow sticker on yourself?

Ed's story is relevant for three specific reasons:

1. It's important for you as a reader to see what the model looks like in person before we go any further in the book. Your self-awareness has to point you somewhere and that somewhere is toward reinvention. Your self-awareness will help you define what you need to reinvent before you are asked to reinvent it— just like Ed did.

2. Reinvention can be a subtle shift leading to significant results. It doesn't have to be a monumental new job or massive project that you nailed. It's about changing the way you approach your work day-to-day.

3. It took time for Ed to truly believe in the model, but when he saw different results from his different actions, he was inspired to try more. Having the courage to really allow oneself to study oneself is a tremendously personal experience. Not different than the exercise for sociology majors watching people who are watching the painting, this mode of observation also triggers giving yourself permission to be more self-aware.

Throughout the years I have worked with hundreds of Ed Cogans. Some of these stories you'll hear as we work through this book together. Each of the stories have different characters with different plots but all revolve around one central theme: **In order to stay relevant you need to reinvent and in order to reinvent you must be self-aware.**

Chapter Summary

Reinvention is about proactively anticipating the need to shift how you create value as a leader. It's a way of ensuring your relevance as a leader and being ahead of the change curve. Self-awareness is what triggers you to know it's time to reinvent.

There are three aspects of the reinvention model:

- Self: Find new skills that make you more relevant than last year.
- Others: Find ways to add value by helping others to be more valuable.
- Business: Find opportunities to upgrade the business before your competition does.

Self-aware leaders know to reinvent before being asked. They take time to observe what's needed and use that insight to adjust their leadership portfolio.

Chapter Three

THE FOUR PILLARS
OF REINVENTION

"If there is no struggle, there is no progress."

— Frederick Douglass, American social reformer, writer

A ttending professional conferences can sometimes be frustrating. Too often, when speakers share a model or philosophy, they fully cover *why* their ideas are necessary, but they fail to give functional advice on *how* to implement them. This book will not make this mistake. Not only will you learn that the secret sauce tastes so good, but you will also learn how to make it yourself.

The research related to the model in this book has proven that each of these pillars will drive your next reinvention. Without these critical skills, you will not be able to fully realize your potential. The four pillars include:

- an above-average network and support system
- a proficiency in critical and systems thinking
- a savvy perspective of the political landscape
- a courageous drive for magis (more for the good of others).

Now, you could stop right here and skip to the next chapter because you've seen the list. You know what ingredients make up the recipe. But then again, if you skip learning how to create the meal of the century, you'd be no better off than sitting at a conference listening to a thought leader tell you why but not how. It would be like taking the answers from the back of your workbook but never really learning how to answer the questions. Getting your homework done quickly works in high school but it doesn't work here.

This chapter connects the foundation of self-awareness to the goal of reinvention through four pillars. Then, the rest of the book defines how those pillars relate to the core model. These pillars are validated behaviors necessary to build your reinvention. In order to truly take advantage of this chapter, you must:

- Work to truly understand what each pillar means.

- Understand what this reinvention looks like (or could look like) in your daily work life.

The goal isn't just to learn them or list them. It's to live them.

Pillar #1: An Above-Average Network and Support System

Being connected is being productive. Building a network is like piecing together any strong team. You have to surround yourself with other productive people. This success demands a variety of players: superstars to utility specialists, veterans to rookies. Yet, few leaders commit to network-building with a similar vigilance. Why? Networking is not just about job hunting or cold calling sales prospects; it's about being connected to be productive.

Remember the old adage, "it's not what you know, it's who you know?" Nobody likes to believe this is true, but...it is. But there's a *huge* difference between an introduction and a handout. The former gets you in the door, the latter gets you what you need. Many people want to see you succeed. It's not a handout, because they won't give you a handout.

They won't give you something you don't deserve. What they will give you, if they like you enough, will be access to opportunity. They will give you a chance to help them grow their organizations.

Leaders today realize that who you know isn't a shortcut to success. It's the most traveled path to success. Effective networks help us turn "what we know" into action. More and more of today's businesses have become interdependent, thus fewer people control their own destinies. You have to invest in building a network of individuals who want you to succeed. And symmetrically, you need to wholly invest in the success of others. You must invest in others not as a leverage in your own career, but because success breeds success.

Networking: You Are Always On

In 2000, Commerce Bank hosted a relatively large recruiting event, to hire 20 branch managers. The core competency of a branch manager is to sell; they need to be able to walk into a room where they know no one and "work it." The event was designed to assess for those exact skills. All 100 candidates were told that the event started at 7:00 p.m. All hiring managers knew the actual program would not start until 7:20 p.m. Why is that 20 minutes important? It allowed the hiring managers to assess how many of the candidates would sit and wait versus how many would press the flesh and kiss the babies. By 7:30 p.m. half of all candidates were out of the running because they did nothing in that 20-minute exercise.

Stop looking at networking as a catalyst, and begin to see it for what it is: your ultimate team. Want a quick litmus test? Run through the following series of questions and see where you land.

- How many elevator rides at work do you need to take before you see someone you "know?"

- When you send an email, do people respond or do you generally have to follow up?

- When you hold a meeting, do people show up? How many of them are peers? How many are more senior members of your organization?

- When you ask for help, how many people raise their hands?

- How quickly do people respond to your voicemails?

- Who are the top three people you call when you need an answer but don't know where to find it? Do others list you on their top three?

The self-aware leader is a gardener, cultivating and caring. They not only plant new seeds, but they also care for the current crop. Networking is a meticulous promotion of growth in others, and thereby the continual renewal of our own status. It is a daily, routine-driven ritual; not a series of happy hour mixers or weekend conferences.

Overall, your value as a leader will boil down to how you treat the people within your network and support system. Ask more than you tell. **Strong networks are a means to information and information feeds self-awareness.** Commitment to the value of such a network will deliver the courage to walk into a room where you know nobody and build rapport, win allies, and create momentum.

To be as plain as possible, people want to help people they like. Strong networks are built the way all relationships are built: with time, trust, and shared interests. People will really listen when and if they really respect you, and that type of relationship can't be facilitated at a business card exchange.

Converging Your Network and Your Support System

There's a saying from the South: "If you ever see a turtle on top of a fence, know it didn't get there by itself." The point is that all leaders (and all people for that matter) need people to push them on good days and lift them up on bad days. Whether it is colleagues, friends, spouses, or mentors, being surrounded by an amazing support system will influence your success. They become vital to your productivity by helping you maintain your momentum.

A strong network can and will guide your decisions and influence your judgment. It will serve as an informal focus group. Leaders that can blend their network and support system take things to the next level. A support system is a much deeper relationship than a network and therefore has a different purpose. It can be trusted completely either on a personal front, professional front, or both. It's the type of person you call on for a trusted perspective in confidence.

Most leadership positions today don't come with binders explaining how to be successful. Whether you are on day 10 or year 10, nothing important is turnkey. Leaders must learn the ropes along the way, and having people you can respect and trust is invaluable. Likewise, having others that respect and trust you turns followership into massive, influential networks. These networks give way to a much more permanent type of power. The power that emerges from a network and support system built on trust and respect and genuine care for one another creates a bond of solid oak.

Pillar #2: A Proficiency in Critical and Systems Thinking

I have consistently benefited from a series of very tough teachers. First, my mother is an English teacher who made summer vacations more academically challenging than regular homework in the school year. Second, my favorite college professor (Mr. Burke) made me write and rewrite paper after paper until I "got rid of the clutter." And finally, my children have been amazing teachers. They teach me over and over that I cannot control everything regardless of how good my idea is or how passionate I am. What do all of these teachers have in common? They taught me to question everything and look at the big picture. They taught me that true understanding is not just memorization. They taught me how to think on my feet.

Seeing What Others Don't

Leaders who rise above the rest don't just see what's there; they read between the lines and see what others don't see. They see the potential answers while others are still harping on the problems. They think on their feet, but also realize that it is just the first step. These leaders go a step further as they dissect complexity. They ask more questions and gain more clarity. They question the obvious until it becomes absolute. They serve as their own risk managers and their own sales managers. They sit on what they think is the right answer until just the right moment. Academics may teach the science of thinking, but experience teaches the art—the street smarts.

There are two types of thinking that drive the success of reinventors: **critical thinking and systems thinking.** The former is a methodology that calls for a constant questioning of the status quo in order to create more substantive solutions. Critical thinking is often perceived as only process improvement or problem solving but can also be a form of brainstorming and idea creation. The latter, systems thinking, highlights relationships between related aspects of an organization by recognizing the cross-functional impact of decisions. For example, if marketing has a new promotion, systems thinking considers the impact to functional teams like customer service and operations. To a large degree, this one-two punch is a combination of left brain/right brain thinking (critical thinking represents the right side and systems thinking represents the left side). Individually, each is strong, but when employed in tandem, a powerful leader emerges.

The Recipe for Dual Proficiency

The perfect recipe for driving dual proficiency in critical and systems thinking includes: three parts data, two ounces of brevity, and a splash of "splash."

Three parts data: Strong cases for reinvention utilize and respond to data. If you ever took a statistics class and hated it, you know that data can often be spun to reflect need. Yet, the reality is that executives thrive off data. Martha Soehren, Comcast's Chief Learning Officer, has a saying: "In God we trust—for all others, I need data." But data is much more than creating or reviewing reports. Critical thinking investigates the data for patterns within the trends. It creates a baseline to measure success against. Systems thinking uses data to realize how change might effect an entire organization. It engages all parties influenced by this change in defining the problem, the desired outcome, and the solution.

Two ounces of brevity: Proficiency must play to an executive's attention span. It must fit within the confines of their desire to talk more than to listen. Maureen Cullen, the former vice president of development at Saint Joseph's University, was a stickler that fundraising proposals be less than one page. She would turn back tremendous ideas because of verbose presentation. Many found this irritating at first, but once the lessons were learned, it all made sense. As Granville Toogood said in *The Articulate Executive,* you have eight seconds before people begin passing judgment on what you are about to say. Strive for brevity. Think of problem statements and the desired outcomes in terms of one sentence each. Executive summaries should never exceed one page. Comcast now teaches middle managers Maureen Cullen's one page lesson. They hate it too…at first.

One splash of "splash": Critical thinking can potentially trap you in a land of perpetual "what if's." Systems thinking analyzes the upstream and downstream impact across an organization. Strong business cases make big splashes, but there's a difference between making waves and making a splash. One key difference: splash is not about *you* being sexy, it's about the *idea* being sexy. For example, the idea may fuel your organization's commitment to diversity or sustainability. To create splash you need strong perspective.

Proficiency in critical and systems thinking is not about employing a specific model. It's about having a mindset that thinks about the progress and growth of an entire organization. It's easy to be blinded by the day-to-day challenges that task you with keeping your head down and getting the work done. The reinvented leader has the courage, strength, and persistence to keep their head above water and look out over the horizon at something new. Once a middle manager makes this adjustment of consistently balancing the strategic and tactical worlds, they never look back. The edge of critical and systems thinking simply become standard operating procedure for them.

Pillar #3: A Savvy Perspective of the Political Landscape

The course of our careers brings us face-to-face with a cast of thousands. There are leading men and ladies, action heroes, character actors, villains, and even walk-on extras with no lines. The roles constantly change, but when the curtain falls, your star power will depend not only on how well you've played your part, but also on how well you've navigated a minefield of egos, sensitivities, grudges, and deception. And that's all before lunch.

Political Work or Political People?

Too many leaders try and categorize politics into two classes: people and projects. They will refer to projects or meetings as being political. The reality is that projects aren't political, the people working within them are. In other words, if Suzanne is working on a customer retention project, it's not the topic of customer retention that is political. It's the fact that Suzanne has to work with Shannon to make the project move. Influencing Shannon is the key to Suzanne influencing customer retention. If Shannon jumps on board, Suzanne can fly. If Shannon is looking to undermine Suzanne, then the fight for power, progress, and success begins.

Politics is intimidating. Not everyone wants to or likes to play in that arena. But shying away from politics is career-limiting. You have to play the game. On the other hand, positioning, leveraging, and posturing for success can make some organizations look like air traffic control rooms. Politics affect project visibility, project funding, obstacles, rewards, and so many other things. Positional power can bring high honors and recognition, but if that power isn't managed proactively, it backfires.

> "Power corrupts and absolute power corrupts absolutely."
>
> **—Lord Acton, *English Catholic historian, politician, and writer***

Office politics, at the end of the day, are surprisingly similar to playground politics. Some kids are picked first for the dodgeball team because they are talented athletes. Others are picked because if they are not picked, they will become angry. Angry kids are likely to expose you and attempt to dethrone you as team captain. You can't change that, so don't worry about it. Instead, seek to understand who is working with and against you. Sure, there are a handful of people who will just not like you and your style—they are likely insecure and thus looking to outdo you. But for the most part, it's more the person's interest in the project. Just remember, it's the person that's political, not the project.

Think about leaders you have seen who are great with frontline employees working in the field. They'll go toe-to-toe with their bosses, their peers, and can easily hold their own. But put them in front of a senior executive, and *bam*, they don't believe they should even be in the same room. They fear the zeros at the end of the executive's paycheck and it's so obvious. It's debilitating. If you fear the executive on the other side of the mahogany desk, then you are less likely to speak your mind, push back on an idea, or even take a risk. This is the difference between successful leaders and forgotten leaders; successful leaders have the courage to overcome the fear and make a move.

Doing Nothing Is an Action

Many Type A personalities work too hard and play only to win. This directly affects what leaders say and don't say or do and don't do as they assimilate into a new role or a new project. One can learn a lot simply from observing others and what not to do when trying to right the ship. It says much about the soul of an organization and which way the tides are going. As Michael Watkins points out in *First 90 Days*, learning and listening is initially more important than acting. The self-aware leader is professionally patient. She understands that sometimes she must slow down in order to move things forward. Everyone warns against being "the ostrich" of your organization. While sticking your head in the sand leaves your posterior exposed, it doesn't hurt to not always be the center of attention. There's no harm in avoiding the beast until you learn the nature of it. Timing is critical. Pace yourself. Manage your desire to just get 'er done.

In the arena of power and politics, biting your tongue is a skill. This is not to imply that leaders should not speak their minds, but it's important that leaders realize that they cannot *always* speak their minds. When your organization's or manager's ideas of success are inconsistent with your own, it can be difficult to keep your inner conflict invisible. Asking the question, "What will success look like?" when faced with any new opportunity, from job interviews to new projects buys you more time to observe and learn. It's important this becomes more than just a "great question." The answer is very important. Whenever someone asks it, he already has a version of the answer in his head. In reality, the question is asking, "So, are our ideas of success the same?" This more professional game of "are you thinking what I'm thinking" can expose disconnects in perception and preempt future conflict. If conflict does exist, the self-aware leader has another decision to make. Does she express the conflict and make it visible, or does she wait?

While there is no easy prescription to offer in this situation as there are too many variables that could influence the best approach, there are some key things to always consider. First, choose battles wisely. Second, decide when and how to speak up based on the potential severity of consequences. Third, know that sometimes the smartest person in the room has the answer but also has the wisdom not to express it. Make the right answer someone else's idea. Sometimes, empowering others to give the right answer is not only good leadership, but it also provides a way to get others thinking about solutions. Great leaders know the answers to their own questions, and know why it's important to ask the question anyway: questions create activity.

Pillar #4: A Courageous Drive for Magis (More for the Good of Others)

This last pillar was my first true love with this model. There are plenty of savvy people who have strong networks, skills, and experiences. Yet, some never see their long-term potential fulfilled. What are they missing?

Being Good for Your Organization

Being "good" at work is not only about numbers or sales or goals. These things may make you an amazing practitioner, but they will never make you a leader. Leadership is about *doing* good *in* your organization, as much as it is about *being* good *for* your organization.

The Latin term *magis* (meaning "more") represents the goodness of service by asking: "What more can I do for others?" While it has religious roots in Suarez as well as the work of Saint Ignatius, founder of the Jesuits, the use of the term here is completely agnostic.

The Roots of Magis

Franclsco Suarez was a 16th century Spanish philosopher and Jesuit priest. Many of his teachings established the foundations for modern Catholicism. The Catholic Education Resource Center synopsizes his core values by informing us that Suarez believed:

"The objective of society Is to optimize the common good. This requires not only an awareness of the ultimate good for humans, but also a means of assuring that the good of the whole does not annihilate the good of some individuals."

Now reread the sentence above and substitute the word leadership for the word society and employees for the word humans.

Think about the most successful people you have met. What do they all have in common? Instead of using a competitive urge to outdo someone else, they are driven by a competitive spirit to push progress for the good of others. This is magis. Magis is as simple as an extended hand. It's an email with background information that wasn't asked for but is vitally important. It's a pat on the back or a heads-up to a colleague about trouble ahead. It's the perspective that we go to work as part of a journey, not as a destination. It's the insight that we are only as successful as we are good—all of us. It's about putting team success before individual success.

To do this well and consistently, one must have significant courage. Why? You leave yourself vulnerable to those who do not value magis. But what if you find yourself in a scenario where your firm's values trump and even define your values? This is what it means to sell your soul to the firm. Self-aware leaders bring themselves into their work rather than vice versa.

The Three Keys to Exercising Magis

1. **Be authentic.** If you don't want to incorporate this value as part of your rules, then don't. There's nothing worse than someone who fakes magis. It will significantly backfire, so look within and make sure you want to commit to this characteristic. You can be aggressive with your career and still be service-oriented. Keeping a corporate eye out for others doesn't mean leading exclusively with your heart. It means that if you make an investment in someone else, you are ok if there's no returned favor. You did it because it helped, and because helping was the right thing to do.

2. **Be intentional.** Magis must be focused on something or someone. It's not pixie dust you sprinkle in the air and hope for the best. Magis requires strategy. Why does goodness matter in this case? This is not meant to create a spirit of Pollyanna. It's meant to be specific. So how do you pick the person or the situation? It's all based on judgment and trust. For some reason you need this person involved to move your work forward. Ask why you got hired into your role versus the other 57 resumes your hiring manager reviewed. It's a calculated risk based on past performance and future potential. But it's also a gut feeling on who will be a good fit and a good team player.

3. **Be committed.** Your belief in magis will be tested the first time someone takes advantage of you. It will be a definitive moment each time it happens. When it does, will you conform to the methodologies of others, or will you find success in ways that stay consistent with your values? It's an individual decision that cannot guarantee it will bring you more money. It may not affect the title on your business card. Yet, magis does have one selfish element: you decide the values to live by. That is where the courage is needed. Courageous leaders stay true to their values and take risks that promote the success of others.

Pints and Leaders

My brother-in-law Chuck is a genius. He never graduated college, but he built his own house. He's that guy that didn't follow the traditional path, never aspired to be senior vice president of whatever, and yet he'd crush you in Trivial Pursuit, and then excuse himself to go back to rebuilding his computer. One of the most professionally fulfilling conversations I ever had with Chuck was when I asked him about his perception of the difference between good and great leaders. His answer, with no hesitation, was "beer." At first I thought he was being a jerk, but then I realized that he was totally serious. He meant that great leaders are the ones you'd want have a beer with—and if you asked them, they actually would.

Go ahead and think for a moment of the people who you have most admired in leadership roles throughout your career. How many of them would truly cherish sharing a perfectly poured Guinness?

Fundraisers quickly learn that people will give you their money before they give you their time. Donors would say here's a $250 check, now please leave me alone for another year. The same thing happens at work. Bosses depend on raises to grow loyalty. The problem with this approach is that research indicates that the excitement of a pay increase only lasts two pay periods. After that, the new salary feels normal, so the buzz is killed. Yet when an employee feels that a boss has taken a "personal interest," the effects can be long-lasting. Again, think back on your favorite boss of all time—would you have left working for her if offered a

10 percent raise somewhere else? Would that have been a good decision 10 months later? Being around good people means more than being paid 10 percent more.

Connecting Self-Awareness, Reinvention, and the Pillars

The introduction of these pillars represents the final step in laying out the visual models within this book. You started by learning the foundation of self-awareness. You then learned that if you use this self-awareness to drive reinvention, you can reinvent in three different ways. This final element connects the two.

The Self-Aware Leader

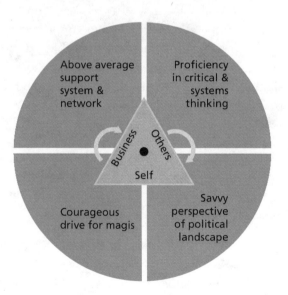

Grow your self-awareness in order to reach your full potential. Work to effectively implement each of the pillars and you will not only see success in your work, but also in the work of others.

	Reinvent Self	Reinvent Others	Reinvent the Business
The Foundation: A strong self-awareness.	Allows you to understand how others perceive you and how that affects your brand.	Allows you to have confidence that adding value to others will add value to you.	Allows you to see how others will perceive the idea coming from you (versus from someone else).
Pillar #1: An above-average network and support system.	Connects you to resources and positive reinforcement on your new direction.	Connects you with more and more opportunities to set others up for success—you are a hub.	Connects you to the right sets of ears that may listen to your ideas.
Pillar #2: A proficiency in critical and systems thinking.	Creates visibility as a generator of new ideas and shows versatility in thought.	Creates a distribution to conjure up momentum for your new ideas.	Creates a disposition that you are in tune with growing the business.
Pillar #3: A savvy perspective of the political landscape.	Paces you past elephants and land mines to your destination.	Paces how and who you align with as friends, enemies, or otherwise.	Paces your drive with when and how to introduce your plan.
Pillar #4: A courageous drive for magis (more for the good of others).	Gives your drive a foundation set in values that are all about creating a better world.	Gives you permission to do good for others with no expectation to see a favor returned.	Gives you an edge that the win for the business doesn't have to be all about you.

Specifically, the research on this book highlighted the following conclusions:

- Self-aware leaders see more job opportunities and more project opportunities than those who are not self-aware.

- Self-aware leaders who are above average with pillar #2 (critical/ systems thinking) see 34 percent more direct reports promoted and 22 percent more promotions themselves.

- Self-aware leaders that also exercised pillar #2 (critical/systems thinking) and pillar #4 (drive for magis) the most had the greatest success building trust, delegating work, improving performance, and coaching team members.

- Self-aware leaders that showed the most proficiency with pillar #3 (political savvy) had the most sense of security with their job and were the happiest with the pace of their career progress.

- Self-aware leaders who were above average in pillar #4 (drive for magis) had a 21 percent higher promotion rate of direct reports and 19 percent higher promotion rate of self.

The strength of this model can come from outcomes like those listed above or simply from the architecture. If you are a student of architecture you know there are many different types of pillars. They come in different shapes and sizes but every pillar has the same purpose—to manage stress conditions. Pillars transfer weight and while some are decorative and others functional, they all have a purpose. The same is true with these four pillars, only they are not either decorative or functional, they are both. Today pillars take the form of studs embedded within walls. You cannot see them but you know they are there.

Chapter Summary

The four pillars of reinvention connect the base of "self-awareness" with the drive for reinvention. Each of the four pillars has been validated by research and together they prescribe the specific leadership behaviors that encompass self-awareness. The pillars are:

- an above-average network and support system
- a proficiency in critical and systems thinking
- a savvy perspective of the political landscape
- a courageous drive for magis (more for the good of others).

These pillars represent the architecture of the leadership model presented in this book. The rest of this book talks about carrying the weight and managing the stress as it exists in today's work world. You now have the model and all of its elements. Now it's time to learn about application.

Section Two

The Application

You have now learned that like everything else, your skills have a shelf life. You also learned that perpetual reinvention drives growth for self, others, and the business. Finally, you learned that the key to this sustained professional relevance is self-awareness—and specifically self-awareness embedded in the four pillars.

The Self-Aware Leader

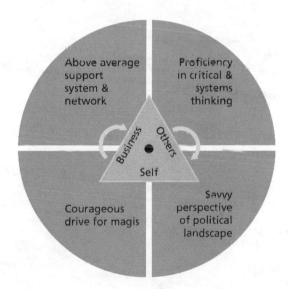

Now the work begins. This section connects the theory to your daily life. If you are a manager, this section introduces prescriptive methodologies for becoming more self-aware and, therefore, a better leader. If you are a training professional, it provides clarity on what leadership behaviors to emphasize in your learning solutions. Either way, you'll want to grab a pen to take notes on how to bring the concepts of this book into your work.

Chapter Four

PROFESSIONAL AUTHENTICITY

"Mass advertising can help build brands, but authenticity is what makes them last. If people believe they share values with a company, they will stay loyal to the brand."

—Howard Schultz, chairman and CEO, Starbucks

Can you really be yourself at work? Think about it. I mean really be you. Or do you hold things back? Is there a "you" that the people at work just don't get to see? Is that a good thing, or do you compromise who you are because you filter yourself at work? Professional authenticity means defining who you want to be at work. It doesn't mean you must be the same person you are outside of work, but it does allow you to choose how much of your true self shines through. It calls for you to stop hiding your best attributes.

So how do you define what is right for you? And how do you do it in a way that allows you to blend in but not sell your soul to your employer? The key is self-awareness. Remember, self-awareness gives you the power to pause and reflect on what you bring to the table. This knowledge becomes power; power for you to make a choice. You must be intentional about who you want to be at work, and you must be secure with your answer before you even consider *reinventing self.* There is no standard answer, but there are standard steps that can be taken toward staying true to self.

Gail From Accounting

Imagine you are driving to work, cruising at 70 miles per hour on the highway, windows up, iPod blaring. You are not only commuting to work, but you are also working your way through the second verse of U2's "I Still Haven't Found What I'm Looking For." It's not just the normal radio version, it's the *Rattle and Hum* live version with a full gospel choir. And you are not just singing; you are flat out performing. Openmouthed, facially expressive, you are giving all of those 70,000 screaming, imaginary fans their money's worth. As your exit looms ahead, the off-ramp is symbolic of not only a change in vehicle speed, but also a more personal transition. The freedom and anonymity of the highway gives way to crowded streets and stoplights. Meanwhile, in your cockpit, the song climaxes, but the show's already over. You're in the public's eye now. It's time to be the professional version of you.

All of us, at one time or another, has felt the conflict of being caught between two worlds. On one hand, you are a mile from the office—you can still be you, right? On the other hand, the coffee-sipping, sleepy-eyed brunette in the car beside you could be Gail from accounting. You don't look directly at her, hoping to avoid the awkward car-to-car smile. Do you wave? Did she just wave? You're not sure it's her, but you can't risk it. You could never let her see you singing in the car. You'd be a water cooler punch line, email forward fodder. That's simply not how leaders act. Or is it?

> **Note to Reader:** We all choose to remain guarded at work. The purpose of this chapter is not just to ask if you are OK with that, but rather to warn you that being too guarded is not a good move. You give up who you are (a person) to be what you are (an employee). Don't lose "you" in your employee role. Instead, learn to integrate the best parts of your more private self into a more progressive leadership brand.

Defining Me

One of the sad truths of humanity is that we are all judgmental. Nowhere is this more evident than in the office. Nowhere are we more guarded about "being ourselves." We are so anxious to fit in, that we risk auctioning off our spirit and originality.

You have faced this challenge before in life. It takes you back to your teens and figuring out who you were in high school. The reality is that today, your office is probably made up of personality types similar to those iconic high school models. You have your nerds, jocks, and cheerleaders, your troublemakers and slackers. Don't sweat it. You're an adult now. Unlike high school, you no longer need other people to justify your identity. You define you. Or better said—you can define you. Yet, much like high school, staying true to this defines courage. It comes down to having the strength to be you rather than being who others want you to be.

Thus you see the great catch-22 at work. On one hand you know that relationships drive success. People want to work with people they like. The fact of the matter is that fitting in is important. On the other hand, professionals often cite establishing a "professional image or presence" as one of the most important disciplines for corporate success. Being different drives the success of brands.

The same holds true for your brand. Your professional brand is not just about the wrapper—it's about the contents of the package. The real you is much more valuable to maintaining a professional balance between your own belief system and that of your organization. Your organization likely teems with people advancing the same reflections of upper level expectation and protocol. But, the spark your organization saw when they hired you belonged to the real you.

Is Your Normal Different Than My Normal?

Everyone has their own definition of normal and that is OK. Everyone is also different and that is OK, too. Normal is what you grew up with and your normal is different than the normal of the person sitting next to you. If your normal was life as *Leave it to Beaver* and hers was like *The Simpsons*, then you both don't define normal the same way. If you came from a big, wealthy, dysfunctional family and she was an adopted only child in a poor family, then again you both see normal as different. If you were in a military family and moved a great deal then your normal is different too. But if you had never really reflected, truly reflected, on how being normal and being different conflicted professionally...you might miss the point.

I missed the point until I spent the day with Stella. I was in a full-day training session in a hotel conference center, and the topic was diversity. Now, having been in training for many years, I've designed, facilitated, and attended my fair share of diversity programs. But as a Caucasian male, I was in for one of the greatest lessons about professional authenticity without even knowing it.

Let me pause here to tell you something important about me. I have always been fascinated by studies on race and gender. As a sociology major, I remember taking course work in social norms and other related topics. I vividly remember, during my senior year of college, reading *The Bell Curve* by Hernstein and Murray about how race influenced success in school.

So there I was, the Caucasian, Irish, corporate gent sitting next to a friend and colleague Stella, the Asian-American, female lawyer. We had been paired up for an exercise by the trainer after finishing a conversation on "white privilege." Prior to the session, we read an interesting article that led to some heated conversation on the current state of racism and prejudice.

Several individuals shared very specific examples of how they had witnessed both racism and prejudice as recent as weeks ago. One

African-American man spoke of being in an elevator when a white woman clenched her purse. He was an executive at a savvy financial institution and the reaction had him fired up. Others shared similar experiences and the lively discussion took off. The trainer, an African-American woman, decided to break the audience of 100 into pairs to answer one simple question. The question for me was "what does it mean to be a white male in my profession?" For Stella, she was asked to answer, "what does it mean to be an Asian-American female in her profession?" I was selected to go first. I was fine with this. I'm a training professional and have no problem speaking in front of people. I design and assign these types of exercises all the time, I thought to myself. No problem.

Except, there was a problem; I was stumped. Then speechless. Then hesitant. And finally, completely silenced. I didn't know how to answer the question. Then the trainer said, "time to switch," and so Stella, mercifully, just smiled and answered. Her answer was precise. Stella was working in a field dominated by white males, and she felt that truth at work every day. She felt pressure to bring more than her true self to work each day because she was a woman. She expressed the details of her emotions and gave me examples of how this had played out. I learned a great deal at that moment. Her specificity and ease with the question. . . the fact that she could answer this question so specifically taught me a great deal. I learned that I was not very in touch with myself. I learned why people of color despise when people say they are color blind. I learned that walking in someone else's moccasins means walking as them in their moccasins, not as me in their moccasins. People of color have a very different situation. And just because I think I am open-minded and inclusive in my thoughts, words, and actions, I should not filter the fact that others don't think, speak, and act the same way.

But professional authenticity is not just focused on the color of one's skin or gender for that matter. The premise of me sharing that very personal story is not about diversity, it is about knowing who I am and how I bring that to work versus what others do. It is about being normal and different all at the same time.

Common Obstacles to Professional Authenticity

When organizations face obstacles, they build new strategies. They learn from past trends and build plans to drive future cycles. Yet, most people don't dissect their career strategies with an appropriate attention to detail. It's one thing to allow last year's successes to inspire this year's innovations. It's another thing to allow last year's mediocrity to drive this year's stagnancy. Leaders incorrectly fuse past successes with projected plans until it all blurs together. Many professionals simply put their heads down and hope for a promotion. Whether your focus is career or business, you cannot look at this year the same way you viewed last year; you must become accustomed to annual reinvention. That reinvention starts with knowing yourself. Knowing yourself depends on authenticity. In other words how "real" are you professionally? Professional authenticity, a term describing the honesty of your professional action, measures who you really are against what you really think and what you really want. The challenge is making sure that the *you* in that last sentence is not defined by others.

For many professional cultures, ideas become squashed because of the power of groupthink, a concept that illustrates how peer pressure within a work group can eliminate conflict by promoting shortcuts to consensus. Many meetings, retreats, even brainstorming sessions are mind-numbingly facilitated in a way that discourages original thought. They are designed to quell, not promote, innovative ideas. Attendees feel muzzled by the notion that going against the grain is counterproductive. We have all felt lulled by this effect. Groupthink kills imagination, innovation, and ownership, but it still seems to find its way to work every day. The boardroom doesn't need to be the "bored" room.

Want some examples? The following is a list of lame, reinvention-stifling phrases that have somehow become universally accepted as decent responses to organizational issues. Coming soon to a meeting near you—the language of groupthink:

"If it ain't broke, don't fix it."

What this supposedly means: If something works well right now, don't waste valuable resources on addressing its function; wait until it breaks.

The groupthink translation has become: Unless something is losing money or causing crisis, don't sweat it. Don't be proactive, just be reactive. Wait until a crisis to do your best thinking. Only fix broken things, don't update old things. If it works today, it'll work tomorrow.

What the self-aware leader should know and do: Leaders should put time and thought into how to keep what works working. They should also not shy away from questioning how to sustain and update great ideas to withstand the tests of time and globalization. That's the crux of the term reinvention.

"What can we do to avoid reinventing the wheel?"

What this supposedly means: Let's not work too hard or invest too many resources into potentially creating something new, when an effective prototype already exists.

The groupthink translation has become: Don't mess this whole thing up and make it more difficult than it needs to be. The shoe almost fits, so wear it and be happy about it.

What the self-aware leader should know and do: People often applaud this sentiment for its efficiency. Yet, it can stifle creative, broad thinking. It implies that all good ideas have already been developed and that a one size fits all patch will neatly cover the hole in your suit jacket. Self-aware leaders provoke debate by tasking teams with the challenge of reinventing the wheel.

"In times like this, it's best just to keep your head down and lay low."

What this supposedly means: You are simply crazy to say or do something that will draw attention to you right now. Do you like making money? Then pipe down.

The groupthink translation has become: Bringing attention to yourself in tough economic times only creates short stories with bad endings. Don't promote change; don't even appear to be thinking about innovation. It scares people. They will walk you out the door.

What the self-aware leader should know and do: Of course, some times are more appropriate than others to be aggressive, but a fear of communicating is a fear of success for high potential leaders. A loss of creative spin usually leads to professional regret. Besides, troubled times call for creative solutions. Have a great idea? Try selling it internally before bringing it forward.

All professionals face these questions at some point in their careers. But these aren't actually questions. They are sometimes threats. They are most often excuses, but they are never productive. Try to recall instances in which these questions pervaded your career. How did they make you feel? Uncomfortable? Reassured? Did you vocalize concern or bite your tongue?

In today's organizations, professionals sing a variety of different songs at work, but not all are in tune. And very few are in unison. If self-awareness of your professional authenticity is such a driver of leadership momentum, be sure you are harmonizing with the right people. Use your experience, your gut, and your values as a guide, and stand back, amazed at how quickly and confidently others join in. You won't get it right every time, but the failures will be great leadership lessons. Finally, learn from watching others to see how certain initiatives work in your environment. As Ralph Waldo Emerson said, "Learn from the mistakes of others, you'll never live long enough to make them all yourself."

Assessing Your Own Professional Authenticity

The search for professional authenticity is a journey, not a destination. Ironically, though it comes from the inside out, professional authenticity is influenced by the outside, and moves inward. We are perpetually influenced by those around us, for better or worse. Sometimes the most negative influence can be the most predictive of our success. Influence can both challenge and fortify our self-awareness. As people come and go from our daily professional lives, we are left to gauge the changes each person makes to our idea of self.

This exercise will challenge you to assess your own authenticity by measuring the most influential individuals in your life. Are these people bringing out the best in you? Or, are they keeping you from authentic self-awareness?

Step 1: In the first column on the table below, list the 10 people at work that most influence your success at work. As you build this list, think about balancing the list with people who you work for (your management), people who you work with (your peers), and people who work for you (your team). You can go beyond 10 names if you are inclined but do not stop short of 10 names.

NAMES:	They treat me fairly all the time	I can be myself with them	I believe they want to help me	They give me very candid feedback	I can tell them what I really think	TOTAL

Step 2: Check on a scale from 1 to 10 (10 being agree, 1 being disagree) your response to each question as it pertains to the individual listed on that line.

Step 3: List the five names with the top scores in the cell marked T1 and then list examples of how you can be professionally authentic with them in T2. Then do the same with B1 and B2 but on the other side of the scale. List the five individuals with the lowest scores and then write down examples of why these individuals were not scored higher.

	T1	T2	Positive Examples
Top 5			
Bottom 5	B1	B2	Negative Examples

Step 4: Examine the trends. Reflect on what is common that you can do with the top five that you cannot do with the bottom five. Note: this does not complete the exercise. Skipping step five is a huge mistake.

Step 5: When you look at what you cannot do with those in the negative examples, does it bother you? Do you feel like it compromises your ability to be you at work?

Step 6: Are there things you chose not to do with either population? Are there things you practice outside of work that you cannot practice inside of work?

You will always work better with some people, and not so well with others. The key to this exercise are steps five and six. You really have to do some soul-searching. No one can really help you with this exercise, and if you do it too quickly, you could talk yourself into a corner. It's easy to convince ourselves that things are fine the way they are. But that's not always the case. Current day, the loyalty of an employee is to their manager and not the organization. If you get what you need from your manager, the rest is more likely to neatly fall into place.

Increasing Professional Authenticity

No one argues with the convention of "be yourself," right? Well, actually, no. When you talk to someone oftentimes, "be yourself" really means "be the more professional you." I remember a direct report coming to me one day just a week after returning from the Center for Creative Leadership. She had attended a week-long program as a developmental opportunity as she had high potential. As she shared what the outcomes of the week were for her, she started to tear up. I paused and asked her what had happened. She shared that she had realized she was putting so much pressure on herself to mirror my style and the style of my boss, she wasn't being herself. She said she now felt free. Free to lead herself. Free to grow herself. Free to be herself. So how do you sustain being yourself over time since you and your environment change every day? There are three main tactics: define what you stand for, understand the currents in your organization, and stand up for what you value.

Define What You Stand for (and What You Don't)

As a senior at Saint Joseph's University, I had the honor of serving as The Hawk—the nation's top mascot as rated by *Sports Illustrated* and *The Sporting News*. What sticks with me about the experience of being a college mascot is how I viewed the world from inside the Hawk suit. It allowed me to become a different person. I had a different face, and so I was protected. I could bring the Hawk to life and was therefore defining the mascot, but in many more ways than I could have foreseen, the mascot was defining me. Being the Hawk taught me that the impact of my actions was not just about me. Self-awareness works the same way.

The same holds true for all of us. Granted, we may not all don a costume and flap 3,200 times a game, but we all choose what we stand for with what we say, what we do, and what we keep silent about. With today's technology, discovering "true self" has never been so complex, or convoluted. Facebook and Twitter lead the social media parade that offers ever-increasing opportunities to present varying degrees of self. Now, your work self and home self is joined by your online self. Less than a decade ago, only public figures worried about their careers ending with a story on the evening news. Now, social media informs recruiters before they finish screening your application. Middle-aged professionals often use LinkedIn for professional networking and Facebook for personal networking, but the reality is that younger professionals don't differentiate. They are who they are, online and off. Social media information is public, and therefore a record of who we are.

One thing I stand for is my family. Fifteen years ago, I worked in an environment where people were judged by what time they got home and what time they left for work in the morning. Today there is no more "off the clock" time. We are always on. Life and work are inalterably fused. I often joke and say that I work shift work. With four sons, I wake up and work before they rise. I work a normal day, and then make it home for dinner with my family and to put the kids to sleep. And then after all are asleep, I log back on and finish my work. Do I get looks when I walk out at five o'clock? Sure do. Do I take pride in those looks? Sure do. I prioritize my family over my work every time. In other words, be aware of who you want to be and be confident and secure in that role. Be professionally authentic. I want to be first and foremost a great father and husband. I want to live by my values, and I want to laugh at work. I want to respect the management team I work for. I want to be able to say what I am thinking, and I want to learn each day, so that I can be better at my profession tomorrow than I am today.

Understand the Currents in Your Organization

Remember Squirt, the young sea turtle from Disney's *Finding Nemo?* Squirt was not new to the ocean. He could swim very well, and he knew the currents. The movie tells the journey of Marlin, searching for his lost son Nemo. At one point, Marlin needs Squirt's help in navigating the Eastern Australian Current (EAC), a powerful, jet stream-like water flow. Jumping in was an important first step, and Marlin had to release his fears to do so. But too often, leadership models preach only the importance of jumping in. They are often quick to tout the merit of "swimming against the stream." But swimming against the flow before learning to swim with it is like running before walking. Original, creative, and progressive thought is important, but it is far more effective coming from someone who understands the flow and order of an organization. Neophyte leaders need a Squirt-like tutorial to swimming within the flow first. Like Australian sea turtles, leaders need constant reassessment and precise timing. They need to know the when, where, and how of a given environment's natural flow. Leadership is not just about having the courage to reinvent, but it's also about influencing others to follow you. Jumping in is a crucial first step, and eventually, innovation is valued, but developing an instinct about an organization's changes in momentum demands self-awareness.

Not a Disney fan? Don't spend your weekends hanging out with preschoolers? Think of this in basic product marketing terms: a gap analysis. If leadership is all about moving from point A to point B, the hardest part isn't either endpoint, it's the line that connects the two.

Jane recently transitioned from a regionally based job to one with a national scope. Three months into the job she recognized the most challenging part of her reinvention. Before, she was at the top of the food chain. At the regional level, she had the final say. In her new job, she had stakeholders in every direction who wanted a say. Jane laughed and said, "I now know what you meant when you said the hardest part wasn't going to be what we have to do, but how to get it done. There are so many chiefs that want to drive my projects. If I don't play to their needs, I won't go anywhere."

The skill that was stretching Jane the most wasn't anything technical. She was an excellent producer and very internally self-aware, but she needed to adjust her self-awareness to account for how others perceived her. As a leader she needed to secure her followers. Jane was learning that there is no value in taking an organization from point A to point B if you do it alone. When Jane shifted her self-awareness from internally focused to externally focused, she was able to reinvent her leadership style. She's no longer a regional leader in a national job. Now, her leadership brand matches her title.

Stand Up for What You Value

Leaders are challenged to be self-aware of both people and tasks. The people side includes professional authenticity. The task side includes prioritization of their work. These self-aware leaders stay on top of existing projects. Generate new sales leads. Focus on numbers and deadlines. It's what gets measured, reported, and compensated. Yet, what more often determined how well these individuals realized their potential existed in how they managed and inspired others. Resist the temptation to view people as simply means to carrying out tasks by living in a transactional world. Recognize people, especially colleagues and subordinates, for who they are, not simply what they are worth.

Leaders are willing to say what needs to be said. But self-aware leaders know when and how to say it. They work on establishing a reputation for saying what others in the room are merely thinking. Workplaces are teeming with people too timid, unsure, disinterested, or inarticulate to point out elephants in a room. Throughout your career, you'll also meet people who have the tact of Howard Stern or Charles Barkley. But while these gentlemen drive ratings on Sirrus Radio or TNT, a leader's ratings can be severely affected by a coarse, brash demeanor. Work on knowing the proper time and place for brutal honesty or common sense solutions. There are times to question and challenge convention. Yet, there are also times to roll with the punches. In other words, strive to be the kind of person who is unafraid to point out spinach in teeth or toilet paper on heels. Whether or not people like it, they will respect it.

Professional authenticity demands an appropriate alignment of your professional and personal selves. Note the word appropriate—find your "normal." What is appropriate for you and your place of work? People want to celebrate their soul, and they want to work for an organization with a soul that shares their values. The 21st century will be known as the time when professionals stopped fearing and started singing. Add your voice.

Assessing Your Team/Organization's Professional Authenticity

Traditionally organizations also have their definition of normal defined by the handful of gray-haired white guys who sit on the executive team. More and more successful business models of the 21st century seem to be those that forego emphasizing image, and instead focus on the human realities of its employees and customers. Just ask anyone in high-end retail. You can no longer determine if someone has the means to buy luxury items just because of what they look like when they walk in the store. They could be independently wealthy or be buying on behalf of someone else. From Timberland and Google, to Trader Joe's and Wegman's, newly viable and financially important companies are trying to send a message to America. People want to be themselves at work. People want to sing U2. The jargony, unproductive Dunder Mifflin-like offices of the 1990s are the satire of the 21st century. The old boys club, chain-smoking, suit-clad, Rolex-lined business model is now the stuff of history books and AMC dramas. The new mantra is identity is everything. Image has implied arrogance; identity is authentic.

Assessing team or organization authenticity comes down to asking the right questions and listening. Employee opinion surveys do this as well as focus groups, but really that's all just working to create an open dialogue. Using the table on the next page, you can establish an organizational baseline and then examine the specific data for as many populations as needed. For example, if you used SurveyMonkey, you could ask these same five questions of your boss, your upper management, your peers, and your direct reports. Or you could ask these questions to employee populations from different interdependent functions like marketing, finance, and customer service.

	Strongly Agree	Agree	Slightly Agree	Slightly Disagree	Disagree	Strongly Disagree
I believe this population treats me fairly all the time.						
I can be myself with this population.						
I believe this population wants me to help them.						
This population gives me very candid feedback.						
I can tell this population what I am really thinking.						

Some people are so insecure that they cannot be themselves. Are you one of them and if yes, what are you going to do about it? This is what reinvention of self is all about. Think you have it figured out? Then be proud and true to where you landed, and help reinvent others by teaching them how you did it. People work too hard and for too many hours for them not to be themselves.

Professional authenticity is about letting people really be who they are at work—as much as they want to. Some find value and comfort in shielding aspects of who they are. Others find it terribly suffocating. It's a very individual decision point and a very personal one at that. It comes down to self-awareness of your values and then takes reflection as well as discernment.

Chapter Summary

Professional authenticity is about bringing as much of your true self as is appropriate. Appropriateness should be based on what you want (not what your employer wants). Self-awareness of your professional authenticity is like brand management for yourself; you need to understand how others perceive you. Other points emphasized in this chapter include:

- Self-assessment on variables such as trust, rapport, and feedback from others is one method to analyzing the professional authenticity you have with others.

- Not bringing your true self to work will negatively influence your personal contentment with work and your ability to productively contribute.

- Reinvention within professional authenticity is about letting you be you—so you can be more productive and more fulfilled. You could also help do the same with others.

Chapter Five

PROFITABLE IMAGINATION

"The most sophisticated people I know—inside they are all children."

—Jim Henson, creator of the Muppets

Organizations must evolve to compete. Departments must evolve to remain aligned. Leaders must evolve to stay relevant. So how do you train your mind to come up with the next great idea? This chapter focuses on a mental framework that gives you profitable and progressive ways to dream. It's an exercise in being commercially relevant. It's the difference between growth and profitable growth. If you are a dinosaur in your thought process, you, your team, and your organization will become extinct. People may admire your fossils but you will move no more. Yet, if you are the new and improved you, people will want you around—a lot.

Think Different

The difference between ordinary and extraordinary lies within a unique combination of three things:

- a hefty imagination that constantly asks "what if"
- a hearty effort that uses raw hustle to push execution over the top
- a healthy dose of good luck.

Imagination truly pushes the ordinary to be extraordinary. If you are old enough, you might remember the first time you saw the black and white Apple Computer posters entitled, "Think Different." They were part of an ingenious advertising campaign in 1997 that featured black and white portraits of people (past and present) who thought outside of the box or who were visionaries in their respective fields. The posters featured everyone from a pensive Jim Henson in full admiration of his creation, Kermit the Frog, to Albert Einstein, Amelia Earhart, and Ted Turner. In fact, the posters are collected and sold today for hundreds of dollars.

Nevertheless, this series of posters says a lot about imagination and discovering possibilities. As children our imagination is fearless. It knows no boundaries. It suggests endless and even irrational possibilities. It exudes the wild magic that can erupt from a simple disregard for routine.

But then we grow up and become adults. Our imagination becomes muzzled. Its once cool, clear, and important voice becomes weird, annoying, and even foolish. Following the voice of our imagination, once a necessity, becomes a stigma. The whiplash effect of adult socialization and daily pressures reboots our hard drives. We program ourselves to no longer think like children. Unfortunately, today's American organizations are not staffed by children, but by adults. Adults who hide their imaginations leave themselves in a state of progressive mediocrity.

Remember professional authenticity? Kermit said, "It's not easy being green." Imagination is not a word many adults would use to describe their strengths—it simply sounds too juvenile. So don't call it that. Call it reinvention.

Leaders need to reinject imagination into the forefront of how professionals think and act. Profitable imagination, thus, is the application of "Think Different." It is an art and a skill that is best led by the power of imagination under the careful eye of the child within us all. It is a principle built to address the vision of Henson, the impact of Kermit, and the evolution of Apple. It neatly melds Darwin's survival of the fittest into Marx's mode of production and creates a commitment to perpetual and selfless reinvention.

Managing Your Brand

Just as Apple has built a brand for their business of reinvention by moving from Macs to iPods to iPhones and iPads as their core product, this book is intended to work with your personal leadership brand in the same manner. Yes, that's right. You, as a leader, have a brand no different than any item in a grocery store. Your brand is something that others either want to buy or don't. For example, when you go to the grocery store with granola bars on your list, it is very likely you have a favorite. Let's say it's Quaker Chewy S'mores granola bars and that anything else is no good. If the store doesn't have the Quaker brand, you drive to another store. Price means nothing. Convenience means nothing. All that matters is brand. You are loyal to the brand.

Your leadership brand is no different. Once your customers, co-workers, or supervisors believe in your service, performance, and values, you will hook them. You will hook them just like my wife is hooked on a granola bar with a smiling Pennsylvanian on the wrapper. They will come to expect a consistence of quality from you—your brand. This consistency of quality will establish their loyalty, and price or convenience will take backseats to the brand.

So, how do you establish and maintain a brand of leadership designed to compete in today's business environment? Cue Kermit, as the answer comes from an imaginative reinvention. The model for reinvention discussed in this book thrives on three core elements: reinvent self, reinvent others, and reinvent business.

Earlier, I discussed the inspiration of Kermit and Jim Henson on this book. Ironically, Henson's legacy became a testament to the importance of empowering and reinventing those around him. Henson met an untimely death in May of 1990 from pneumonia at the age of 54. The tragic suddenness of his loss presented myriad obstacles for Henson's production company. Foremost was the fact that Henson never taught anyone how to perform Kermit's voice, leaving one of the world's most iconic characters literally mute. The loss of Henson almost led to the loss of Kermit, and although Henson's son taught himself how to give life to the famous frog, the transition was long-coming. It was thus very obvious to the public. Immediately following Henson's death, the public cried out to be comforted by an appearance from Kermit. No one could perform the voice, and Kermit's absence only punctuated the tragic loss of his creator. Inspiring and mentoring others may be the most important step in preserving our legacies. Point in case, will Apple be able to sustain their profitable imagination without the leadership of their founder Steve Jobs? If they don't, will it tarnish his legacy?

Profitable Growth

Many organizations are lulled into complacency by repeating the same pattern. At some point, organizations need to wake up. William Taylor, the founding editor of *Fast Company*, often refers to it as the "practically radical meets radically practical." Not every culture can tolerate his use of the word radical, but his spin on things supports the premise of profitable imagination. If reinvention is the innate ability to merge imagination and execution, then leaders must think critically and act courageously to grow.

Now, it's one thing to daydream—it's another to envision. You cannot simply reinvent the business with ideas; you must be able to generate action and growth with the ideas. They must be profitable. So how do you do this? And what if you don't consider yourself financially savvy? The first step is to think about this organizationally, not individually. Let me explain.

> "If you properly use your imagination it will help convert your failures and mistakes into assets of priceless value; it will lead to discovery of a truth known only to those who use their imagination; namely the greatest reverses and misfortunes of life often open the door for golden opportunities."
>
> **—Napoleon Hill, The Law of Success**

Hill's quote promotes the power of imagination, but the tool is only positioned in reaction to a negative experience.

Profitable imagination capitalizes on pillar #2 (Critical and Systems Thinking) and pillar #4 (Courageous Drive for Magis). It does so in a way that takes the proactivity of the reinvention model and simply asks "what if." It asks questions that drive improvement. This may seem simple, but is actually a huge challenge for most organizations.

Most leaders instinctually attend to what is failing publicly. Most are unwilling to play with the magical formulas that drove success. Reinvention starts a new story before the last one is finished. Thus, it's almost as if the leader never actually finishes the book. To a degree this condition could be labeled a sort of Executive A.D.D. This reference contains no disrespect to the medical condition of A.D.D.—it is a challenging disease that negatively affects many people. But a limited attention span can fuel reinvention. Think about it—if you have a limited attention span, you probably start more things than you finish. Are you the leader that puts things in motion and empowers others to execute? Or are you the leader that comes up with the great idea and sees it through to completion, serving as the primary driver? Both send two different messages of value for you as a leader. There will be more on that in later chapters.

When you think about working at both for-profit and nonprofit organizations, there are clearly positives from both sides. Though so many people vocalize the differences, there are exceptional commonalities. Growth drives the success of each. Even a highly successful organization cannot be exactly the same from year to year. If it is, success won't last, because its customers or donors won't stick around. Sure, people love tradition, but people also love to be connected with a winner. And winning comes from growth and change.

Financial leaders often speak about the principle of being a commercial enterprise. These enterprises are in business to make money. Solid fiscal foundations for growth benefit customers, employees, and shareholders alike. Today, the term profitable growth is used a lot because growth in and of itself is worth peanuts unless it contributes to your organization's financial stability.

> Profitable growth challenges today's organizations to have the soul of a nonprofit but keep score like a for-profit.

Today's CFOs measure not only the product that sells the most, but also the one that makes the most. For example, if widget A makes .25 per unit, but widget B makes .50 per unit, most analysts would commit resources to the growth of widget B. But what if widget A sold twice as many units? These types of decisions can plague today's leaders. Answering them will dictate how Wall Street evaluates your organization's growth. It's also how you should evaluate where to invest your energy and money moving your business forward, regardless of whether your widgets are donors, students, or projects.

Yet, too many organizations are shortsighted. Leaders aren't differentiating between growth and profitable growth. Leaders are being pushed to attain "more," without defining what "more" means to the bottom line. But, if you want your organization to be a leader in its industry, as well as be around in 10 years, you need to grasp the financial drivers of your work. This applies to all leadership, whether you are leading an organization of $20 million in revenue or a team of 20 employees.

Two Philosophies on Profitable Growth

A 2004 *MIT Sloan Management Review* article entitled "Building Ambidexterity Into Organizations" is a tremendous teaching tool. The article points out how value comes from seeking new opportunities (adaptability) or streamlining existing efforts (alignment). Either of these approaches can fuel profitable imagination. Whether it reduces expenses or produces revenue, whether it is old news or new news, the reinvention is there for the taking. But will you wait for a lull to respond? Or, will you seek out a time to progress? Everyone is trying to create the next great widget. Proactively managing your brand is about proactively managing your business.

Think of something you are working on today—make sure it's a deliverable and produces revenue or decreases expense. Got it? OK, now research the patterns of data around that topic. What is your company data telling you? Does what you are looking at have a shelf life? How do your competitors stack up to that data? Ever hear of Yellow Tail wines? They were created to convert beer drinkers to wine. That's adaptability in action. How about UPS and being able to track your package? That's alignment to decrease costs in the form of customer contacts. Profitable imagination calls for very creative thinking but it can come from outside in or inside out. Some are new ideas and others are new ways of executing on existing ideas.

Adaptability	Look outside the current state for new opportunities
Alignment	Look inside the current state for efficiencies

Four Ways to Increase Your Profitable Imagination

1. Be clear on how you currently create value and ask if you can exercise other methodologies.

If you go back to thinking about yourself as a brand, then your value is quantified based on what you produce. Good brands sell more than bad brands. The same is true here.

- If you are great at defining and even anticipating what work needs to be done next, then you are a **leader**.

- If you are great at getting the work done but need the scope handed to you, then you are a **manager**.

- If you are great at getting people to agree but don't produce the actual work, then you are a **facilitator**.

- But if you are great at creating a tangible output, then you are a **producer**.

Using those four definitions, list below the top 3–5 projects you are working on today. Then answer which of the four roles you primarily play within each project.

Top Projects	Leader	Manager	Facilitator	Producer
1.				
2.				
3.				
4.				
5.				

The obvious point of this exercise is that the role you play in each of your projects aggregates into your current brand. There is no right answer, just a question of whether you are comfortable with your answer. The less obvious point is that you have an opportunity to influence what role you play going forward on future projects. You can have that dictated to you, or you can start doing the little things today that position you for that new role tomorrow.

2. Imagine what can be done, not what cannot.

The main difference between adults and kids as it pertains to imagination is that adults have learned what "isn't possible." It biases everything they do, creates fear, provides distraction and yes, even gets people promoted. This is not a proposal to be careless. This is a statement to attest that careful imagination can drive success. You have to be able to see what others cannot and then pull them in. Get them excited to the point where they feel goose bumps. Rally the team around a mission and then let them crank it. Sure, they will think you are a bit crazy. . . but is that all bad?

This will work more easily with some populations than others. For example, sales organizations are often highly motivated by massive challenges. They are willing to take on just about anything if you give them the right tools and incentive program. They visualize success. But, if you have a highly technical population, this will be tough! The engineers of the world are trained to go first to why it won't work. Finance leaders may only see the hard numbers. Use questions like, "So what's it going to take to make it work?" and over time they will embrace the approach.

3. Work backward.

OK, so now you have this mind that won't stop thinking about new ideas. You're wondering how to channel it—how do you make it profitable? You must start by working backward. Joe Laipple, PhD, from Aubrey Daniels International created a model in his book *Precision Selling*, where he teaches leaders to start with the customer.

Simple, narrow-minded organizations start with asking "What are our goals?" And in most cases the answer is a simple metric that drives sales, customer satisfaction, or revenue. Sophisticated, open-minded organizations start by asking: what are we trying to get the customer to do?

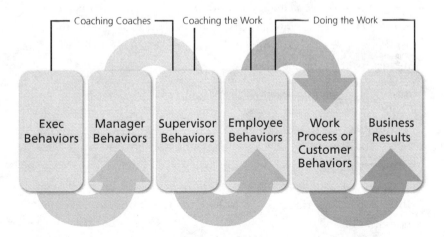

When Comcast launched On Demand as a product, the most difficult things about selling it were that (a) many customers fear advanced technologies and (b) they fear intangible technologies even more. In this case, On Demand is a library made up of content that is 95 percent free. As the product launched, Comcast was challenged by how to teach customers how to use On Demand via 30-second advertisements. At that time, it was foreign to think about an online library of movies.

When we took the crew of high potentials through this exercise of working backward, their inclination was to focus on the customer seeing On Demand as the technician installed the product. Here's a small but very important point; the key to this was what customer behavior drove the intended result. Seeing was not the behavior that would drive repeat use of new technology. People fear technology and once it beats them they won't use it again. The key to changing customer behavior was for the technician to have the customer try it while they were in their house. This gave the customer confidence that they could use the technology all by themselves. This shift in customer behavior was instrumental.

Now, profitable imagination is not just about coming up with the On Demand product. Profitable imagination is about working backward and changing the customer behavior. How's this for a fact? As of July, 2011, customer downloads of Comcast On Demand exceed customer downloads of Apple iTunes, and both products were launched a month within each other. Granted, the two products are different technologies, but it gives you a sense of how modifying the customer behavior affects the success of a product rollout.

What does profitable imagination look like in other industries?

Hospitality — How do you get hotel customers to *not* ask for their sheets and towels to be cleaned? Blame the environment. It takes housekeeping extra time and drives costs. Launch a massive green campaign and guilt customers into doing the right thing for emissions, while also doing right by your budget. This initiative saves hotels thousands of dollars a day.

Mobile Phones — Why is it legal to distract yourself with lighting a cigarette while driving, but it's illegal to use a hands-free on your phone in more and more states each year? The answer involves money. Think of the hit the tobacco industry would take if you couldn't smoke while driving. Further, the government has mandated safety features like air bags and seat belts, but hasn't it missed an opportunity with Bluetooth?

Gambling — How come no one offers a subscription service for state lotteries? Sure, there are severe problems with gambling addictions, but that doesn't stop states from conducting lotteries. Millions of people would easily pay $5 a month to be included in all drawings for an entire year. That's a no-brainer.

Retail — The District of Columbia now charges any customer from any retail store a five cent plastic bag fee. If you ask your checkout person for a bag, fork over a nickel. Political figures came out of this one looking "green" and "saving green." In one year, this program decreased the number of plastic bags from 23 to 3 million per month and raised $150,000 in incremental revenue for environmental cleanup.

Transportation — Most states now have some version of automatic toll payment. Drivers prepay for tolls using a credit card and can slow down instead of stopping for a toll. Even rental cars now leverage this cashless system. This business model cuts down on labor needed to staff the toll booths. Why not have people retake their driver's test every 10 years? This could increase revenue for the state and take some lousy drivers out of the picture.

In 2009, when *Forbes* produced the list of the top 30 innovations in the last 30 years, it wasn't a surprise that all of the top 30 were dependent on technology for their origin. The top four were: Internet, PC/laptop computers, mobile phones, and email. You don't have to be an engineer of the actual technology, though; you just have to have the foresight to dream what the new technology could do and how it would benefit the customer and your organization.

4. Validate that your approach is truly profitable.

Profitable imagination is about a curiosity that truly entertains anything as fair game: broken or working, new or old, hot or cold. Imagination has no bias. It is not easy. It is not linear. And it is not risk free. But does it positively affect profitability?

- Know who keeps score at your organization, how they keep score, and who is winning or losing.

- Repeat the item listed above. It's that important.

- Read, listen, and learn. The more you know, the more you can imagine. Allow your mind to wander, but make it a productive, purposeful wandering. Everything you come across has a point. It relates back to your work. It must add value.

- Take time for your mind to slow down. It's like any other muscle. Rest time is just as powerful as maximum stress time. Have lunch with people who see things from different directions and have them help test your hypothesis.

- Think like a kid. Remove any ideas of limitations. This helps you break out of conformity and see things for what they are and what they could be. Ask why like 17 times in a row to question the current state.

- When mom says no, go ask dad. Know that like anyone in product research or sales, you often need to go through nine no's to get your yes. Stay committed to the exercise.

Will You Share Your Dreams With Others?

There is perhaps a fifth way to increase your profitable imagination:

- Make an intentional decision if it will serve you better to create value through self or others.

But this is not a requirement, it's a stylistic approach. Plenty of leaders master having a profitable imagination without playing it out through others. It's all a question of what they want to be known for.

Your brand is a personal decision that is no different from the car you drive. But what you decide definitely says something about you. Earlier in this book, we talked about the reinvention triangle. If you recall, you need all three elements of the triangle in your portfolio all the time. But you can arrange the emphasis—it just needs to be intentional. If you only focus on self, you could run the risk of abandoning others. If you only focus on others, people may wonder if you are truly capable yourself. If you only focus on the business, people will admire your mind but nothing else. The interdependence of the three is what makes the model, and you, more attractive as a leader.

Reinventing Leadership

A story that blends together profitable imagination and professional authenticity has its roots in Wilmington, Delaware. John J. Raskob was a successful businessman from the early 1900s who was a financial executive with DuPont and General Motors. He was also the chair of the Democratic National Committee (1928–1932) and a prominent opponent of President Roosevelt's New Deal. Raskob had a belief that everyone should invest $15 a week in the market, and this was at a time when earnings per week hovered right around the same amount. Profitable, right? Crazy, maybe? But what is tremendously interesting about Raskob is what he did with his money. He inspired an architect to build the Empire State Building by standing a pencil on its eraser and asking how high you could build it without risk. Then, he took his earnings and created the Raskob Foundation; a family foundation focused on funding causes supported by other Catholic charities.

The current chairman of the board of this foundation, Pat McGrory, is the great grandson of Raskob. When you ask Pat about his experience with the board, he immediately dives into how challenging and rewarding it is to walk into a board meeting with 50 of his aunts, uncles, cousins, and so forth. Raskob erected a family foundation as strong as the building he designed. His vision to construct such a family bond stems from his self-awareness. He knew what he wanted. The board meetings are like family reunions and they stay true to their patriarch's focus. Raskob made something and that something grew. So clearly there's a connection between profitable imagination and growth. You can look at it in terms of dollars, followers, customers, and so many other terms.

> "Go ahead and do things, the bigger the better, if your fundamentals are sound. Avoid procrastination. Do not quibble for an hour over things which might be decided in minutes. However, if the issue at stake is large, stay as long as the next man, but go ahead and do things."
>
> — *John J. Raskob*

Chapter Summary

Profitable imagination is the focus and practice of dreaming for dollars. It ties closely to pillar #2 (Proficiency in Critical and Systems Thinking) as well as pillar #4 (Courageous Drive for Magis). The latter spurs thinking of "the more" and the former creates the connection to the current state. Three key themes to take away from this chapter include:

1. Reinvention calls for looking at the patterns of how score is kept and then dreaming within that infrastructure.

2. What you dream of and how valuable it is to your organization influences your brand just as much as how hard you work.

3. Laipple teaches us that working backward can pinpoint a focus that directly will influence our customer and their behaviors.

Much of what comes from a profitable imagination can come from you. You need to think different and study different. You need to be intimate with what the data says and how technology can reshape your work.

Chapter Six

GENEROSITY QUOTIENT™

"When you learn, teach. When you get, give."

—Maya Angelou, African-American author

The term *giving* has been reinvented. No longer will it only be narrowly defined as a charitable term. People will think of it well beyond visions of UNICEF boxes sounding of spare change or writing a check to fund The Race for the Cure®. Giving is part of leadership. Think about specific people who have made a difference in your professional life—odds are they gave you something. They gave something of value. They gave for your benefit. They gave with no expectation of a return give. This chapter examines the art of giving as a leadership tactic. The premise rests on the fact that people want to work with and for people who give them more than they could give themselves: career growth, happiness, feedback, challenge, whatever it is. This chapter introduces a model and profiles tactics for how you can give in order to produce more in your work.

A New Way of Giving

If you talk to enough people in middle management, you realize that many feel trapped by their jobs and financial obligations that grow with each passing day. The stronger players start to hit a groove with performance as well as compensation and *bam*—they find themselves in a vicious cycle that they cannot break. A cycle of dependency on income levels that fuel comfort. But amidst this career progress they are lacking something else. These leaders are trapped into a focus of filling their wallets more than filling their lives. No, they're not modern day yuppies, they just get into a rhythm of biweekly paychecks and don't want to give that up for a better job with lesser pay. Their time for generosity and philanthropic giving is sacrificed for the grind of chasing career moves that increase growth and earning power. And when they have that low moment where they've had it with the hustle and bustle, many corporate managers today are saying, "If only I could just go work for a nonprofit I'd feel better about my work."

More recently the same conversations are surfacing with middle managers in nonprofits. They want better pay and a quicker pace but aren't willing to sell their soul to a dot-com. Both populations feel they have more to give. Both populations aren't getting exactly what they want from their job. Both populations are frustrated, feeling empty and stuck. So a simple case of the grass is always greener on the other side, right? Wrong!

Managers crave giving something to others and just haven't found a way to make it intentional in how they work each day. This kind of generosity has nothing to do with traditional charity and the giving of money. It's about giving and connecting with those sharing our professional life.

Every day, leaders have an opportunity to give co-workers or those individuals they manage critical visibility, information, or constructive feedback, or just an encouraging comment about a small or large success. It's not about being a mentor to others or a coach. It's about human connection and giving others a sense that what they do matters. All it requires is that a leader be secure and:

- have something of value to give

- be willing to give without a need for anything in return.

Why is this important? Two generations ago, loyalty of an employee was to a company. Today, based on dot-com busts and recessions, everyone knows someone that has been let go. That someone may even be more talented than you are. Giving is important because it creates followership. Without these followers you have no leadership, just a cool business card that means you have a nicer office than your team.

Give Me a Break

In chapter 2, Generosity Quotient™ was described as one's ability to give. If IQ measures cognitive ability and EQ measures the ability to perceive and manage emotions, then Generosity Quotient™ is a leadership strategy that draws on others to increase impact. It exercises actions such as giving opportunity, giving ideas, giving time, and giving support.

You might be thinking that this is something like an organizational group hug. This is not the case at all. The focus of a Generosity Quotient™ is directly connected to productivity and profitability. It's about getting the most out of your people because they believe in you and don't want to let you down. When you show understanding and use your intuition to give someone a chance, or provide advice or help that changes a life, you've used your Generosity Quotient™ in a positive way and displayed generosity at work. There's no fluff in that at all. It's about optimization, like spraying WD-40 on a rusty old bike chain.

Nonprofits have known about the power of generosity for years and for-profit organizations are just now recognizing the power of generosity. The great ones all use the same approach:

- Hook people in—let them feel goose bumps when they become engaged.

- Get them addicted—so much so that they regularly need their fix.

- Have them recruit others to get involved—an early form of crowdsourcing.

The same tactics used for engaging donors work tremendously well with engaging employees. An organization recruits others to get involved and leverages the involvement to drive innovation. With a staff of less than 25 people, Wikipedia quickly realized that in an Internet-savvy world, mass production wasn't dependent on employees alone. Wikipedia opened its doors to its customers to run the business. eBay leveraged this same model, and the result was unexpected and unprecedented growth for both. The difference was that eBay made millions and thus a new business model was born. Then the model was adopted by more "mature" organizations such as Proctor and Gamble and IBM. They all followed Wikipedia's example and began growing their businesses by using social media to involve thought leaders and customers.

Today's companies aren't creating employee loyalty primarily via compensation, but rather by giving more people a voice in the organization. *BusinessWeek* awarded Nissan one of its top innovative company awards in 2011 for its LEAF™ automobile, "the first mass-market, all-electric car." In an interview with the magazine, CEO Carlos Ghosn revealed that the 350,000 employees were at first very resistant to the idea of focusing on electric cars. He said he got past the resistance by making the employees "feel the passion, vision, determination, and focus." The CEO didn't promise smooth sailing either. "I didn't say it was going to be easy or safe," Ghosn admitted. In the end, Ghosn told the magazine that he succeeds by connecting the employees to the dream and honor of being the first major car company to mass market an electric car. "If someone could do it," Ghosn told his employees, "it would be us."

The Generosity Quotient™ Model

The self-aware leader recognizes that *giving* creates a more trusted network and thus a more sustainable leadership style. The Generosity Quotient™ promotes trust among your employees, direct reports, or team members because *you* are a valuable part of *their* network. It shows you don't have to call all the shots, take all the glory, or be the poster child of success. It requires leaders to be secure in who they are and know that any one member of their team could in fact be more successful than they were. For so many years generosity was viewed as a weakness—you gave in. Today giving is a leadership tool. Leaders who recognize this in themselves have a massive step-up on those that don't. The value they can create is not solely dependent on them producing the next great idea or working the extra hours.

Generosity Quotient™ creates leadership value through four types of primary giving. Each of those four types are briefly described below based on what they are, why they are valuable, and how to enact them.

Giving Opportunity:

What: You create chances, visibility, and momentum for individuals to gain access to other people through strong work.

Why: Success is as much about you winning as it is about the team winning.

How: Give up control to get control by delegating so that others own it.

Giving Ideas:

What: You see, sense, or think something that someone else doesn't and you share it for the benefit of others with no expectation of anything specific in return.

Why: People want to be around and work for the smartest person in the room, but only when he doesn't act like the smartest person in the room.

How: Whisper in someone's ear and let them (1) run with it and (2) know that you never had this conversation.

Giving Time:

What: You make yourself available to teach people about data, systems, history, and culture so that others might have the context you have.

Why: People don't want to just be asked to execute; they want their leaders to slow down and explain things so they can be more and do more the next time.

How: Slow yourself down and remember all the people that gave you time when they were too busy and that the brand of being too busy to talk is not a good one.

Giving Support:

What: You tell people what you are really thinking to help set them up for future success. You communicate with candor because you believe in that individual.

Why: People want to have a rapport with the people they work with and for. They want to believe you hired them to make them successful, not just you.

How: Read the patterns of people and recognize when they are not themselves so you can show you care and help lift them up.

The model is simple in that it is extremely intuitive and yet profound as it becomes very telling where one may be strong or lacking at displaying their Generosity Quotient ™. You can use this model not only to manage how you give, but also to define what you need to get from your network.

What's interesting is how the blending of the four types of giving creates four types of givers. By combining support, time, opportunity, and ideas, you produce a specific outcome for your giving. The four types of givers are champions, catalysts, coaches, and confidants. They each serve a specific purpose and potentially these givers don't even come from the same purpose, but all add value to your growth and success as a leader. But rather than list the what, why, and how for each type of giver, let's look at the model in action and learn from a real-life experience with the model.

The Generosity Quotient™ Model in Action

I lived this model firsthand when my manager and friend, Brian Mossor, set me up with one of the most amazing development experiences of my life. Brian did whatever he could to raise me up and told whomever he could that I had strong potential, and those efforts on his part still pay me dividends to this day. Brian was my **champion**.

One day Brian set me up with a mentor from the University of Pennsylvania. Brian asked me to meet with John Eldred, PhD, whom I very much admired. John taught in one of our high potential programs. At one point early on in our mentoring relationship, John suggested I look into the White House Fellowship program. While I had never heard of the program, after 10 minutes on the website, I was obsessed with the idea. John triggered this valuable idea. John was my **catalyst**.

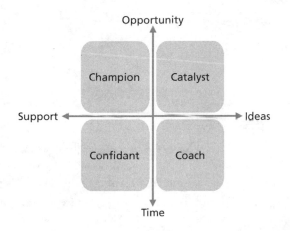

I had dozens of meetings inside and outside of Comcast to gain support for my application. Sheila Willard, senior vice president of government affairs, pulled me aside at a key moment to provide advice on who to meet with and how to introduce this idea. She presented insights that I would have totally overlooked. Her role was behind the scenes and she wanted no credit. Sheila was my **confidant**.

As part of the application, I had to collect five letters of recommendation. One person that immediately came to mind was Col. Rob Gordon, then senior vice president of civic leadership at City Year. Rob and I were close colleagues and I knew Rob had worked at West Point and in the White House, so I saw him as a strong reference. When I reached out to Rob he began to chuckle. "Dan," he said, "I'm not sure you realized that I was a White House Fellow and not only will I write you a recommendation, but I'll also mentor you to help you prepare your application." Rob was my **coach**. He had been there, done that, and was now going to take me under his wing.

The experience of applying for the White House Fellowship program was everything I imagined. I didn't get the Fellowship but I did get everything I needed. Each of these four leaders taught me something very distinct about giving. Each in their own way helped increase my self-awareness.

- The **champion** gave me confidence.
- The **catalyst** gave me momentum.
- The **confidant** gave me patience.
- The **coach** gave me perspective.

Increasing Your Generosity Quotient™

So how do you increase your Generosity Quotient™? If you remember the Comcast 360-degree data highlighted in chapter 1, you see how much the lows are rooted in control, delegation, and trust. Three of the five lowest behaviors are delegation. The reality is that this list is not just about control, delegation, and trust; it's about connecting with others to do those three things.

Shift from managing the work to managing the people doing the work. If you want to really give, you have to realize that you cannot simply give work, tasks, and projects. That is only half of the deal. You must give them inspiration and options and opinions, so they are more than Rosie the Riveter. Think about how you run your staff meetings and your one-on-one meetings. Do you go through their list of projects and do you spend equal time on each project? If leadership is about teaching, not fixing, then you cannot be a taskmaster.

Performance management creates highly productive, low maintenance, self-sufficient employees. The highly productive piece is obvious—your employees must create much more value than they cost to employ, or you should just hire consultants. Low maintenance means that your employees don't have too high of a contact rate. No different than a call center, your time is money and time you spend working with your employees is time you are not working on other things. Self-sufficiency is about coming to a decision point and having the confidence to know which direction is right. This confidence is directly correlated to the low maintenance factor.

To do this effectively you have to think about setting your *employees* up for success, not their projects. If you set them up for success, their projects will follow suit. The inverse is not always true and therefore you can't go betting the farm on great project success. It's high maintenance and will only take you so far—plus it will irritate your employees to no end.

Realize that high control builds low trust. Many of us are control freaks or recovering control freaks. We want people to do their work as we would want them to do their work. Leaders don't realize that the key to getting "the best" out of people is inspiring them to do their work their own way, and allowing their way to challenge and foster the leader's own ideas and plans.

Too many organizations still use a very controlling approach to running their operations. This control monopolizes the growth strategy and feeds egos, not empowerment. The independent business watchdog website Glassdoor.com does an annual survey of the "50 Worst Companies to Work For." To accomplish this, they solicit anonymous 20-question satisfaction surveys from any employee willing to share and publish their findings. A survey of the surveys shows, with overwhelming margins, that the largest complaints do not come in the area of remuneration. Instead, respondents were most upset about—you guessed it—how senior management treats them. The 2010 king of pain: Gibson Guitars. Close to 100 employees responded to the tune (get it?) of 1.8 out of 5 satisfaction, and only a 14 percent approval rating of CEO Henry E. Juszkiewicz. Over and over, employees described work conditions as "draconian," "stifling," and "unfair." Meanwhile, a look over the salary portion of the surveys found the salaries at Gibson to be competitive, even above average. The lesson here is that people will not blindly follow a paycheck.

Create a culture of giving. In the early 1980s, Jane Golden started the Philadelphia Mural Arts program as a way to compete against the city's graffiti crisis. Jane recruited graffiti artists to become mural artists. This was no small feat for a petite Caucasian woman. Most of the graffiti artists were also gang members. But Jane knew that artists won't deface other artists' work. She worked to understand the gang leaders and knew that once she converted a few, they would convert the others.

Today, Philadelphia is the mural arts capital of the world. And what's fascinating to hear as you tour the city with Jane is how she has to prepare the artist. You see, the artist only gets to control half of the paint brush; the community controls the other half. The artist can start with a vision, but they need to be inclusive of community leaders to capture their vision. They need to collectively own the work of art and once they do, the impact is significant. A painted wall leads to a cleaned up yard in front of that wall which leads to filling potholes in the street next to the yard. Slowly people become invested in their community and social change happens.

Share the paintbrush. If you are the only one painting, you can only accomplish so much. Share the brush and teach others to paint, so you can amplify your impact.

How does your team interact with each other? Do they share information with each other? What stops them from working across functions more efficiently and effectively?

Generosity Quotient™ Assessments and Exercises

The definition of management is getting work done through others. Despite this fact, too many of us spend the majority of our time being professionally selfish. We want to control everything and by doing so, display a lack of trust in others. People definitely struggle with this point. It's a huge factor as to whether a leader can grow from managing frontline employees to managing other managers.

Below are four of the most common struggles as indicated in research. Listed next to each are recommendations on how to address them.

Common Struggles	Questions to Help You Assess Self
Owning it exclusively. vs. Getting help from others.	• What are the three things I am most effective at accomplishing? Why aren't others as good at them as I am? Should I be teaching someone else? Should I be including someone else in my thinking pertaining to these issues? Should I hire someone else who is also good in this area? • Why am I not relying more on others in this project? Is it an issue of control? Is it insecurity? Will the team be less productive if I were to leave? How would that change my legacy? How would that affect the organization?
Do it yourself. vs. Delegate to others.	• What is driving me to want to do it myself? Visibility? Lack of trust that others should do it? How will that lack of trust affect team dynamics in other areas? • If I took the length of the task and divided it by the cost of the salary for the person doing it, what is the cost to complete the task? Is the organization overpaying to have this task completed? Am I doing someone else's job because I won't hold them accountable to do it?
Use your voice. vs. Use someone else's voice.	• What is the point I am trying to make? Why does it have to come out of my mouth? • Have I already delivered this message? Am I frustrated that the response has been neutral or negative? • Are my emotions getting the best of me (and the other person) in this situation and would I be better served to make my point through someone else?
Who should I trust more? vs. Who should I trust less?	• Who are my allies in this initiative? Who is neutral? Who is opposed? Are the opponents friendly or are they potentially malicious, territorial, or even insecure? • How can my professional skepticism guide me in whether I should (a) leave this person at arm's length and just be aware of them or (b) call them out and understand my motive for not trusting them?

Chew on these questions for a moment. Now let's run through two small exercises. The first one is introverted in that it asks you to reflect on self. The second, however, is extroverted. It will shift perspectives and ask you to focus on others.

Exercise 1

Think of three significant projects or initiatives you have worked on that tested your leadership skills over the last year. Try and pick one project that went really well, one that went OK, and one that was a challenge. For each of the following statements, respond with either "always", "sometimes", or "never" to indicate how you performed on that specific project.

The next step is to go back and look at the patterns across behaviors and projects. What patterns are you seeing? Are they consistent across the high-performing projects and the lesser? There's no magical score as a result of this self-assessment, only instrumental data to reflect upon. The self-aware leader reflects often and on the right things.

	Project 1	Project 2	Project 3
I allowed others to run project meetings.			
I shared decision-making responsibilities with all.			
I deflected credit to others on the team.			
I had to be present for progress to happen.			
I was the voice for project communications.			
I initiated the ideas that were implemented.			
I shared information with multiple players.			
I spent time with key individuals outside of meetings.			
I shared my belief that the team will drive success.			
I recognized others more than I was recognized.			
I was indifferent about who owned the best idea.			
I valued input to drive stronger solutions.			

Exercise 2

In no specific order, list the 10 most significant people who influenced your success on the three projects from the previous page. This list may closely mirror the exercise you did earlier in the chapter about professional authenticity, but odds are the list of 10 won't be exactly the same.

Now look at the image of the model again. Write the initials for each of the 10 names listed above next to the quadrant that best depicts the value this resource provided you. After this exercise you should begin to see the patterns. The key point of this exercise is to see if you have names in each of the four quadrants. If you do, then your network is providing you with a diverse pool of givers. If you don't, then you now have a reason to network strategically and expand your support system for specific purposes.

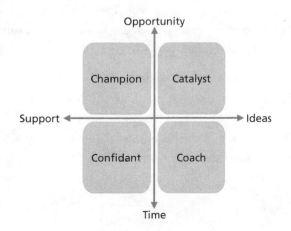

What aspects of the model do you have in your portfolio? Where are your needs? The output of this exercise is better self-awareness of what you need and who can help you get it. Likewise, you can think about your own leadership brand in the same terms. What are you known for and is it multifaceted enough for your leadership brand to be sustainable through change? Only you can answer this, but odds are, if you don't have at least two of the quadrants strongly marked off, you have some work to do.

Giving won't solve everything. Giving can fall short or worse yet, expose you. Not everyone will smile with dimples, thank you, and tell everyone what a splendid person you are. Arrogance, insecurity, and downright ignorance will still rule some days and some people. But don't stop. Instead, be aware that a substantive thought process precedes giving. Stay true to your values and take the proverbial leap of faith. Sure, it does expose you but what great wins don't come with some level of risk? You know what you value, so only you can determine if the leap is worth the risk. You may not see a return every time, but that's not why you give, right?

The Piggyback Ride

Many cities across the Unites States have a local civic leadership program like Leadership Philadelphia. The goals of these types of programs are to work with corporate and nonprofit leaders to better understand how their city ticks as well as how they themselves tick as a leader. Toward the end of this program, teams are tasked with a service learning project. If you have ever done substantive service before, you know that sometimes you go in expecting to give, when really you are given so much.

One April day we found ourselves chaperoning a class field trip to the circus. The students were participants in an after-school program for children with incarcerated parents. As we roamed the parking lot to view the animals outside, a young boy, who was about five feet tall, African-American, and about eleven years old, asked me for a piggyback ride. I thought to myself, "Sure, no biggie." He leapt up on my shoulders and whispered in my ear, "My daddy gave me piggy rides before he went to jail."

That little boy gave me much more than an opportunity to give him a ride; he gave me perspective. This perspective breathed the spirit of Generosity Quotient™ as a leadership tool. We give to someone to help, to take a break, or to have some fun. We give so that we learn more about ourselves and our co-workers each time we give. These lessons tend to sneak up on us. We go into the game with a plan to reinvent self and then we see the opportunity to reinvent others. Done successfully, giving influences each of us to be better people and better leaders.

We all have something to give. . . it's a question of how, when, and why we will give. It has nothing to do with making people like you, and it's not about being the hero. Giving fuels an organization's prosperity. It's contagious and healthy. It helps leadership get the most out of their people by empowering employees to give to others.

Chapter Summary

If you believe in the concept of Generosity Quotient™ and you believe that management involves getting work done through others, then go ahead and give. Here's a reminder of why:

- You may be talented, but you as an individual can only do so much. If you are willing and able to give to others in the form of feedback, information, opportunity, and ideas, you create more value.

- Successful practice of the four areas of giving listed above lead to positioning yourself as a champion, catalyst, coach, or confidant. Be self-aware of which fits your brand. Be self-aware of including at least one of each in your support network. They are essential to building an intentional plan for growth.

- Exercising Generosity Quotient™ empowers others to find success. Sure, there is risk, but when calculated, it gives others a voice. By delegating to others rather than controlling their decisions, you build capacity and trust.

Chapter Seven

THINK LIKE
A GENERAL MANAGER

"Action expresses priorities."

—Mohandas Gandhi, political and ideological leader of India

General Managers (GMs) have total responsibility for all aspects of the business. They may not own it, but they certainly own responsibility for the people, decisions, and results that encompass it. Leaders at any level can learn how to think like a GM. When they do, it's proven to be better for them, their teams, and their organizations. This chapter highlights why you should start thinking like a GM and how to do so effectively. Thinking like a GM allows you to see the upstream and downstream impact of decisions you make and directions you take. It by no means assigns you the authority over those ancillary areas, which is where a leader must assert influence in order to make an impact. Thinking like a GM does shift how you think about success, change, and profits.

How Do You Define Success?

In 2002, a group of 30 senior leaders asked to participate in performance management training. These executives were part of Comcast's highest growth area, Comcast-Spectacor. They possessed strong, positive, results-oriented skills and contributed to a successful culture. Spectacor was looking to push the business and the leadership to the next level. They needed to grow into the types of leaders who were capable of shaping their direct reports into leaders. It was a textbook case of rolling things out top-down and all of them seemed to be generally excited about the initiative. After this training was completed, the game plan was to train all of middle management on the same content. If someone had stopped and asked these executives if they were truly collaborative and connected parts of the Spectacor whole, they would've adamantly agreed. But, after just one icebreaker, they found themselves in for a big surprise.

Each individual was tasked with taking a sticky note and writing down, as a "bumper sticker," the answer to a simple but profound question: "How do you define success at Comcast-Spectacor?" The reaction from the participants was very interesting. Some quickly took pen to paper while others fell into deep thought. Either way they were asked to express their thoughts in a phrase no longer than a bumper sticker. At the end, one truth rang loud before anyone ever spoke—no one had the same definition of success.

Now these were all very smart, very successful executives, but clearly something was amiss. The Finance lead defined success in terms of dollars. The Sales lead in terms of ticket sales and sponsorships. The Human Resources lead in terms of people. The Marketing lead in terms of. . . well, you get the drift. They were defining success in their own eyes—in terms of their own function. And the reality was this definition of success was directly related to the reports they spent the most time analyzing.

The group spent 35 minutes discussing how such an outcome was both good and bad. It was a positive that these executives were laser-focused on their scope of responsibility. It was dangerous though that their focus blinded them to the rest of the business. The participants became self-aware that a shift was needed.

The Four Buckets Exercise

The initial point had been made, but had it truly been embraced? The next day, when these executives returned to their desks, and their dozens of unchecked emails and voicemails...all waiting to embroil them in the troubles of their specific departments...would they remember to "make time" for more global thinking? Would they actually remember to care about the business as a whole? Would it change how they led their teams?

To ensure retention of the initiative, another step is added to the icebreaker. Each of the 30 executives in the room was asked to work with each other at their tables. They were in groups of six, and they now had ten minutes to look at each other's bumper stickers and compress their list of six into a list of four.

As the exercise came to a close, but before they were totally finished, the tables were combined into teams—three tables per team. Each team had an extra 10 minutes. The intended result of the exercise was that each team created one answer to the original question: "How do you define success?"

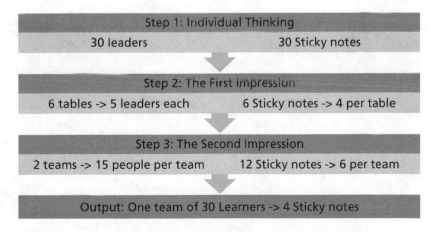

Step 1: Individual Thinking	
30 leaders	30 Sticky notes

Step 2: The First Impression	
6 tables -> 5 leaders each	6 Sticky notes -> 4 per table

Step 3: The Second Impression	
2 teams -> 15 people per team	12 Sticky notes -> 6 per team

Output: One team of 30 Learners -> 4 Sticky notes

This level of detail provided leaders with a framework approach to thinking like a GM. Consolidation of the groups bred common understanding. As leaders better understood the thinking of their colleagues in other areas of the business, the more they became fascinated by the whole.

This exercise always produces the same four buckets—profits, products, service, and employees. And each of the buckets always has the same core focus based on the sticky notes within it.

- **Products** is the output.
- **Profits** is the value.
- **Service** is the customer experience.
- **Employees** is the employee experience.

Spectacor even redesigned their performance management tool to require all employees to have goals in all four buckets. The result was initiatives like those listed in the table below where people had embraced thinking, planning, and even measuring progress cross-functionally.

	Products	**Profits**	**Service**	**Employees**
A Club Box at a Flyers Game	Tickets, food, beverage	Revenue per ticket sold, renewals	The How Ya Doin' program, customer surveys	Employee satisfaction
A Marketing Campaign for Disney on Ice	The campaign	Tickets sold vs. leads generated	Family friendly experience	Alignment between marketing and sales
A Sales Presentation to a Prospect	The pitch	Sales revenue	The experience of the potential buyer	The experience of all affected by the sales cycle

Excited by the responses from the Spectacor population, the unanswered question was could the four buckets model be applied to other organizations. Was it possible that this approach had a broader application? The answer was yes.

	Products	**Profits**	**Service**	**Employees**
Comcast Cable	Video, voice, and internet products	Subscriptions and advertising	First call resolution, customer guarantee, JD Power Survey	Employee opinion surveys and voluntary turnover
Your High School	Teachers, course offerings, sports	Budget per student	The impact on the students	Experience of faculty and staff
Your Favorite Pizza Joint	Pizza	Cost of production vs. cost per slice	General customer service	The culture of the work environment

But most people don't run their own business. They run a project or even part of a project. So how do the four buckets apply to a project? Same approach.

	Products	**Profits**	**Service**	**Employees**
A Process Improvement	The process upgrade	The value of the process upgrade	The ease of implementation	The response by those affected
A New Training Program	The training content and delivery	The cost per completion, ROI	The speed to market, client satisfaction	Employee opinion surveys
A New Product Launch	The product	The revenue	The ease of doing business	Employee product knowledge
A Performance Management Tool	The coaching conversations, goals and the review	Differentiation with merit distribution	How well the tool works for employees/ managers	Response to more time for planning /reviewing progress
A System Implementation	The software	The efficiency the software creates	More efficient customer experience	Just in time training for software launch

Utilizing these four buckets is not about pulling out a wallet card and taking others through a formal process of defining each. It's about seeing the business as a system—and thus the need to be self-aware of systems thinking. This lens allows you as a leader to see the bigger picture. It focuses the self-aware leader on how this initiative will affect products, profits, employees, and customers. The approach can be used proactively to plan or reactively to process. Once adopted, this four bucket approach becomes very natural and provides a simple and clean mental model for how you think about everything.

Four Ways to Think Like a GM

Build Cross-Functional Love

Maura is a Pittsburgh native with strong self-awareness. In 2006, Maura was selected to participate in a Comcast high potential program. It was a challenge for her to reinvent self, others, and the business. It was a challenge for her to question 29-year-old habits and to figure out how to achieve new levels of success. Maura opened her mind to thinking differently and acting differently. After conversations with her manager and her mentor, she was determined to reinvent something. But what? Then it came to her. A simple phrase, no longer than a bumper sticker slogan, was uttered by Maura's colleague, and she was forever changed. Three words: **cross-functional love**. It wasn't something she was used to hearing in any business environment, let alone at Comcast.

Maura was managing a business that was in a ton of flux. New products were being rolled out. New processes had to be defined to support the products. Employees wanted to do a good job but were excited, confused, and overwhelmed. The changes were definitely seen as the right thing to do but making the changes a reality was not going as planned.

Maura began to talk to her peers from other departments about what was working and what was not. Her approach was informal focus groups with a standard list of questions and a commitment to herself to not solve or defend within the focus group. As she aggregated the feedback, one big change people were commenting on was the number of new departments; each department had their own goals. The missing link had been discovered. The departments were all working for a common goal, but the goal was by department and not as a team of departments.

No different than the executives at Spectacor having their own definition of success on the sticky notes, the Comcasters in Pittsburgh had department goals that didn't mesh well with other departmental goals. People were well-intentioned and working hard but not cross-functionally aligned. Maura had now defined the problem but needed to dig deeper for potential solutions.

Maura had learned in Comcast's leadership program how research shows that management creates 85 percent of the issues that cause frontline employees to not achieve productivity goals. To further diagnose this situation, Maura conducted more focus groups but this time with groups of frontline employees. Her goal was still to see what was working and what was broken, but this time she wanted to engage the group in reinventing the business. Maura had now become a facilitator of change rather than just a manager of it. She led by asking questions of each department. How could they work together, cross-functionally, to improve their daily tasks? How could they further affect the customer experience and Comcast's bottom line?

This process opened Maura's eyes to how reinventing the business and reinventing others can work together. She naturally started to think about the four buckets—products, profits, service, and employees—but as it related to the whole system, not just her department. The effect was very different from a single process or technology change. It was a complete cultural shift for how all Comcasters—supervisors and employees—viewed their jobs. They were now all thinking like GMs by virtue of all striving to achieve common goals.

Organizations like Vanguard force cross-functional love by asking all business unit leaders to rotate every 2–3 years. At one point they had an accountant who was leading Human Resources. Wawa, a $5 billion dollar convenience store that Forbes ranked in 2010 as one of the 50th largest private companies, has done this as well. Their Chief Marketing Officer used to be their Chief People Officer. This may seem crazy, but it drives global thought. It proves to the entire organization that success is not a solitary mindset. A self-aware leader does not hinge success exclusively on hitting her own budget numbers. Cross-functional love is a potent first step, but it alone won't generate leaders who think like GMs. Collaboration and alignment are a start, but the reinvention must go deeper.

Critical Thinking Is Critical

Some people live by the mantra "If it ain't broke, don't fix it." Your mantra needs to be, "If it hasn't been broken in the last six months, BREAK IT!" Critical thinking causes leaders to question everything. Self-aware leaders should have opinions on everything. In terms of critical thinking, start by completely de-emphasizing the negative connotations of "critical." Critical thinking is a skill that allows individuals to have the courage and confidence to thrive, even in ambiguity. Reinventors embrace uncertainty with the same confidence they display in more lucid times—with leadership. Having the courage to function in ambiguity creates high levels of intellectual stimulation. This type of stimulation sometimes scares people, especially board members and upper-level executives. Even the most naive new professional knows that can be a bad thing. So how do you both embrace critical thought and avoid career suicide?

Think of all the people you know who are busy at work, but no longer feel challenged. **This is a major career trap: work keeps people so busy they don't have time to realize how professionally unfulfilled they are. People become addicted to being busy.** We must learn to identify and annihilate business environments that promote business as busy-ness. When busy-ness trumps reinvention, everyone gets hurt. Reinventors must operate on a sense of creative optimism.

Here are two stats to consider:

- The Gallup organization estimates that 70 percent of American workers are disengaged, and disengaged workers are dramatically less productive, creative, and committed than engaged workers.

- 42 percent of white-collar workers say they aren't entrepreneurial, citing few incentives for risk takers. (*YouGov/BusinessWeek* poll of 721 office workers on August 4-6, 2008)

Disengagement comes from checking your brain at the door and having to obey orders as commanded by the management hierarchy. It's a passive form of groupthink. Critical thinking increases engagement as ownership for decision-making is pushed to the organization's lowest level. This bucks the age-old trend of driving large decisions upward. People at all levels need to be ready, willing, and able to reinvent self, others, and the business. Leaders need to have the discipline and the courage to know what to reinvent and when to reinvent it. Some of it is skill, some of it is luck, but all of it comes from having the mental framework of critical thinking. Trust in others accelerates careers. The tendency to do things yourself and micromanage situations can be debilitating.

Critical thinking is not something you can learn overnight, but here are the basics on how to think critically:

- **Be paranoid in thought but not in action.** Curiosity can lead to daydreaming but paranoia will drive you to decide if action is needed.

- **Ask probing questions that get to the root cause.** President Reagan used a leadership approach he called "trust but verify." This methodology called for asking multiple tough questions, in order to dig below the surface and learn what was really going on.

- **Assume your competition can do it better.** If you think competition may force you to lose market share fast, this assumption will push you to innovate faster than planned.

- **Brainstorm ways to do it faster, better, cheaper.** Ask your customers and your employees what they would do if they had the magic wand to change things.

- **Ask if killing the initiative is better than continuing it.** Examine the amount of effort on a project as compared to the return for the business. Would anyone really miss it?

Know When You Need to Engage Specialists vs. Generalists

The Philadelphia Chapter of the Society for Human Resources Management (PSHRM) is a 1500 member organization that is one of the top five largest chapters in the country. In 2007, it had a solid board, solid balance sheet, and solid brand—but no growth strategy. Composed of only HR professionals, the board underwent a massive transformation. Under new leadership, the executive board decided it was time to grow. They defined a goal of creating a budget reserve, increasing chapter activity, growing membership, and hiring an association manager. Affectionately known as BAMS to the PSHRM board, it was an exercise in analyzing what processes were in place, how money flowed through the chapter, and where energy was being spent.

The existing board quickly realized it had two challenges: (1) it was spending the majority of their time in the tactical mode and (2) having all HR professionals on the board was a limitation. Knowing that growing the chapter meant having the right type of board in place, the executive committee agreed to significantly shift who was on the board. The recruiting process began and the end result was a financial advisor as the finance chair, an advertising agency leader as the marketing chair, and so on.

There are times when the work calls for "athletes" who have that incredible professional stamina and agility. These athletes can do just about anything you throw their way. But there are also times you need a specialist; someone with the exact experience for the task at hand. Effort and experience have a very interesting working relationship. The PSHRM board was very successful with their growth strategy. It created an infrastructure that has checks and balances in place to sustain any changes in leadership or to veer away from any bad leadership. Could this have been done with all HR professionals? Maybe, but it was definitely not as likely and not as likely to happen that quickly.

The self-aware leader makes intentional decisions about staffing teams and running projects. The self-aware leader understands the full work ahead of the team, not simply just the task at hand. The ability to think like a GM will better inform a leader as to what skill sets are specifically needed. The inclusion of the right mix of generalists and specialists allows the leader to not only trust in her team as people, but also to trust in her team as functional experts.

Respect the difference between positional and influential power.

One of the pillars for being a self-aware leader is a "savvy perspective of the political landscape." This perspective is critical when thinking like a GM, as your positional power may not align with your influential power. Stated another way, your thinking may be more than your title gives you access to or permission to comment upon (see definitions below). This becomes challenging because in your new focus on thinking cross-functionally, you are also starting to look at how others run their departments. Then you start thinking critically about how other department leaders could run their businesses better. The result is you start to look at other leaders' turf. And you are looking at their turf without being asked to do so, which is not always welcomed.

Positional vs. Influential Power

Positional power is what comes with a title. If you are the vice president of customer service then you are responsible for that function because of your job, your title, and the responsibilities assigned to it.

Influential power is much less linear or literal. It comes from building success or momentum. If you are that same VP of customer service, your influential power could be about how you persuade the Finance group to resource your team or the sales group to position you with customers.

If you have the magis pillar in your portfolio, and you are working toward "more for the good of others," your intentions may not always be received as such. It stinks but it's true. A leader's passion for upgrade could be misinterpreted as negative or malicious. In some cases, it's a result of the insecurity of other leaders, and in other cases it could be due to the fact that you didn't canvas the idea first and are now exposing the weaknesses of others. Regardless, it can be rough waters to swim, but this "healthy friction" is what can propel leaders, teams, and organizations from good to great.

Healthy Friction

"The world needs such original thinkers who define situations, fearlessly grapple with conflicting ideas, and discern the possibilities for action. If we seek to teach anything here, it is to recognize that we live in ambiguity; that we must learn to function within that ambiguity.

The university campus is a forum for competing and conflicting ideas. In our conversations when we are in dialogue, dialogue that inevitably reveals ambiguity, conflict, and a thousand shades of gray, we come to grasp the truth. The more comfortable you can be in that ambiguity, the deeper your grasp of truth, and the greater contribution you can make.

The poet John Keats not only acknowledged that conflict in the world, he embraced it. Keats created the term 'negative capability' to describe 'when a man is capable of being in uncertainties.' He found that ideas in conflict created the moment and opportunity for creativity."

Georgetown University President John J. DeGioia 2002 remarks to the Phi Beta Kappa Society.

Remember, people who always try to "fix" other people's challenges are not always the same people who get invited to happy hour. Thus, reinventors must learn to separate the person from the problem and handle each situation differently.

A key element in overcoming this hurdle, and therefore a key element to critical thinking, is humility. In 2002, around the same time that John J. DeGioia delivered the Georgetown speech, Comcast began to embark on an integration strategy for the upcoming business acquisition of AT&T Broadband. It was a case of the minnow swallowing the whale and the goal was to maintain the systems, structure, and culture of the minnow's organization even though, in certain cases, that meant taking a step backward to move forward. The term, positioned by management as the acquisition's theme, was "quiet confidence." It meant going into the integration with a great sense of humility. Comcast needed to understand that while their margins and business models were more productive than AT&T's, arrogance was unacceptable. Comcast leadership had to respect the history and brand of AT&T Broadband, but most importantly, Comcast leadership needed to respect the people of AT&T Broadband.

Throughout this integration, leaders were expected to have an active red pen to edit what others were doing. Yet, people who constantly "red pen" the work of others, at some point, will stop being asked for help. Unless we approach tasks from the perspective of helping others instead of promoting ourselves or our businesses, true growth cannot occur. The leadership at Comcast often explains this as taking the business seriously, but not taking ourselves so seriously.

People take pride in their work. The vast majority come to work wanting to do a good job. No matter what your intention, if you look to devalue some of their work, odds are it won't always be celebrated. The self-aware leader embraces the concept of partnership. Partnership is humble leadership in action.

Chapter Summary

Thinking like a GM explicitly drives reinvention. It is a logical foundation for reinventing the business. It causes a leader to think more broadly about her work and how it gets done. To do this more effectively, call upon the tenets of profitable imagination. The self-aware leader utilizes her imagination and ability to look across the entire organization to envision profitable growth. Thinking like a GM will also allow her to inspire her team to think more broadly as well.

We know for a fact that every action causes a reaction. For leaders, inaction also causes a reaction. What a leader does (or doesn't do) to teach her team to think more broadly is directly correlated to her willingness and ability to reinvent others. Thinking like a GM is a perpetual mindset designed to get more done with less in a way that doesn't depend solely on the leader's narrow realm of influence. It drives productivity down to the frontline and it creates professional opportunities and fulfillment for others in doing so.

Leaders who think like a GM specifically:

- **Build cross-functional love** in a way that has teams thinking about organizational success before team success. This breaks down functional silos and creates common goals for multiple departments to target.

- **Think critically** about the business without being critical of the leaders who run it. It requires leaders to perpetually ask questions about the current state with the goal of creating a stronger product.

- **Know whether a challenge calls for specialists or generalists.** The former has a specific set of skills and experiences while the latter is a utility player that is good at a variety of things. The self-aware leader makes this an intentional decision based on what needs to be accomplished and how involved they will be in the work.

Chapter Eight

FEED A FAMILY VS. SOLVE WORLD HUNGER

"In trying to defend everything, he defended nothing."
—Frederick the Great, King of Prussia

In this hyper-competitive world, everyone is trying to outdo everyone else. Today's leaders have daily judgment calls to make. Will you turn left or turn right? Will you paint it blue or paint it red? Will you launch products to market quickly to beat your competition or slowly to assess any product bugs? The questions are plentiful, but the million dollar question is how much is too much? Pressure on the individual leaders who call the shots is greater than ever. The pressure to win is as intense as the pressure not to lose. So what has science taught us about defining success? The practice of pinpointing, or narrowing focus, plays a critical role. It teaches leaders how to under-promise and over-deliver.

In this chapter, you will learn how to use judgment, science, and precision to clarify priorities. *Solving world hunger* is defined as scoping a massive project way too broadly. An example might be saying that your project is to improve customer service. Whereas *feeding a family* is defined as having a very specific focus for the project: for example, improving the customer experience for one specific product line within the first 100 days. The difference may seem slight but this difference puts the leader and their team into perfect sync. It dramatically increases the likelihood of success.

Scoping the Lift

Too many individuals and organizations attempt to bite off more than they can chew. Whether it is defining goals for the year, clarifying a new focus of a revamped project, or mapping a productivity turnaround, promising too much all at once can be dangerous if not disastrous. Even if they meet or partially meet oversized goals, it's hard to call the result winning.

Self-aware leaders maintain a finite focus and precise goals. This does not mean leaders should not be progressive or aggressive. It just means they should identify exactly what they want to be aggressive and progressive about. With a precise focus, leaders can build career-defining momentum even when achieving small wins.

Comcast's Action Learning Project

A leadership principle of *feed a family versus solve world hunger* is a cornerstone of the Comcast high potential leadership program. The program involves a community investment service learning project where the participants ran a service project to learn more about themselves as leaders. The program design was based on the premise that volunteers are more difficult to manage than employees. Employees are required to follow you. Volunteers follow because they believe in you and your cause.

Leaders were initiated to the idea of community service by attending a service learning project at Children's Hospital of Philadelphia during their training experience. With this firsthand knowledge as background, the leaders were tasked with returning to their respective home market areas and creating a community investment project of their own in local

Comcast markets. Two instrumental lessons were taught as the leaders scoped out this project:

1. *Define the specific family you want to feed before you define the solution.* High potential leaders generally visualize success before the other folks sitting around the conference room do. This type of speedy processing is both a blessing and a curse because the definition of success may not match up to the immediate need. In the case of this project, leaders from the Comcast program went home and approached community-based organizations (CBOs) in their own areas and opened the conversation by saying, "Do I have an opportunity for you" before even listening to what the CBO leaders needed or was appropriate for the organization. This approach was highly unsuccessful and it allowed the leaders to confront their "control freak" and "doer" mode and learn firsthand that leadership and doer-ship are not the same.

2. *Recognize your eyes are often bigger than your stomach.* Have you ever gone food shopping while hungry? You generally will come home with double what you expected. The same holds true for scoping projects. Leaders get excited and have visions of taking the hill like Mel Gibson in *Braveheart*. Passion trumps reality if it is not kept in check. But the self-aware leader knows that over-promising dilutes focus and diffuses momentum. If your realistic goal is to achieve 50 of something (units, new hires, rollouts of new programs, for example) and your hubris and enthusiasm pushes you to tell the public that your goal is 100, what are you going to say when you achieve only 75? While raising expectations is often a good thing, the result, if you don't make your goal, is that you will be remembered as someone who fell short of their goal. The group of Comcast leaders also fell victim to this understandable tendency to over-promise and to think unrealistically, and expended half of their allotted eight weeks for the project before realizing their project had not gotten beyond the planning stage.

Still, the community investment project taught some big lessons while pointing out fundamental leader flaws. The self-aware leader understands that it's tempting to increase a goal once you are ahead of schedule, but they know that decreasing a goal mid-project is deadly for a career.

The lessons were clear to the participants when it came to scoping projects:

- Pinpoint success by identifying the specific (a) employee population, (b) customer population and (c) business process you are working with.

- Recognize it does take a village to get work done, but your work doesn't need to save the entire village in one single day.

Target vs. Bull's-Eye

Here's a business maxim you can live by:

- If you look at problems generally you will drive general success.

- If you look at problems specifically you will drive specific success.

This is a lesson that the Comcast leaders learned from participating in the community project initiative. The leaders recognized they needed to frame the work on the appropriate target and the bull's-eye is an easy way to visualize the process.

If you are in a leadership role, generally speaking, you should be able to define the target. Let's say you are managing a project team of seven people who all report to seven different supervisors. From conversations with others and your own observations, you realize your productivity challenges are based on one of three hot topics:

- the need for better communication

- the need for increased sales

- the need to generate a quicker turnaround time.

You conclude that better communication is the number one priority. That's the family you want to feed. So good, you are done, right? No. This target is still not nearly specific enough. It could mean so many different things. For example, better communication could mean:

- proactively communicating problems as they arise

- sending regular weekly status reports

- having open dialogue with peers

- stronger articulation of the vision for the new project.

So exactly how will you know what approach to take? This will likely be way too big for you and your project team to conquer. By focusing on the main issue and going deep to the root, you can precisely define the focus in a way that is much more manageable. You can plan the work to address the most needed area of better communication. If this effort is successful, you can expand your focus to other areas beyond your initial focus. Leaders need to be able to pinpoint and prioritize work. The self-aware leader just does it better.

Crafting Problem Statements and Desired Outcomes

So you now have the family you want to feed and you also have a bull's-eye. Now you need to define success in a way that positively affects all involved in the project. To do this you have to translate the bull's-eye into a problem statement (PS) and desired outcome (DO) statement. This puts the bull's-eye in writing. This is a bit more difficult than it may sound because people are seeing the bull's-eye from different perspectives, but once you nail it and have all agree, the mission is clear, focused, and intentional for you and your team.

The steps for successfully converting your concept into a specific scope of work include:

1. *Always start with data.* More than a gut feeling needs to exist to take the leader from the target to the bull's-eye. The bull's-eye needs to be justified. Why did you pick that specific bull's-eye? How did you choose the family you are looking to feed? How did you prioritize that need as more important than other needs? You may need to analyze reports, conduct interviews, build surveys, or facilitate focus groups, but you are going to want to have two feet to stand on other than your own. Those feet are data.

2. *Put one self-explanatory sentence in writing.* Next you need to be able to communicate the current state and the desired state in one sentence each. So many leaders convince themselves that this is a luxury, not a necessity. The art of crafting these two sentences will bring more than focus. It will spark healthy debate about verbiage. Struggling for the perfect word will allow you to really hone in on what's important. Cutting unnecessary language will predate cutting unnecessary components. Plus, careful crafting of the focus allows various stakeholders the opportunity to provide varied opinions on finding the right words.

3. *Eliminate any assumptions, double barrels, or causes.* These two sentences should just be about the facts. No information should be included on what is causing the current state (real or assumed) and there should only be one bull's-eye, not two. Bringing a second factor in complicates the focus and then complicates your chances for success.

4. *Build the DO to mirror the PS.* In grade school, you were taught to never define a word using that word. Not the case in writing a PS/DO. You want to use as many of the same words as possible. If you are talking about one specific sales growth metric like repeat customers, let that be the focus, not new customer acquisition. If it's a revenue metric, stay with revenue and don't confuse it with

profits. Changing words from the PS to the DO may change the focus from apples to oranges or something less obvious like Granny Smith to Winesap apples. You want to stay focused on the same metric or outcome in both statements.

The PS/DO Exercise

So now that you've learned what ingredients go into the PS/DO, your next task is to see if you can analyze whether examples are well-constructed. Can you pick up on what is missing in the examples below? See if you can identify what is missing from the statement before you read the issues of the PS listed in the second column.

PROBLEM STATEMENT (PS)	ISSUES WITH PS AS-IS
Over the last six weeks, sales from new customers buying our red product have dropped by 20 points.	What is the start/end date for those six weeks, and is dropping 20 points leaving us at above or below our goal year-to-date?
Between 1/1 and 5/1 the number of new product rollouts affecting our web platform has tripled and we have not been able to train anyone.	There are areas of focus here—product rollouts tripling and not being able to train anyone. Which is right? More importantly, are either of them the actual problem?
For all of Q1 2012, the average revenue per customer that buys multiple orange products in the California region has doubled from $50 to $100 (goal is $64).	Well done!

Some of you may be looking at this as a writing exercise and not as a leadership exercise. It is both. It's a writing exercise because you have to choose your words carefully. But it's your leadership that will guide you as to what words to choose. Here's a clue. You can use the following fill in the blank as a template approach to writing your PS/DO. It may not fit 100 percent of the time but it has all of the essential ingredients.

Now the current state is defined. Assuming all your stakeholders agree with the statement as it is written, you can move on. Odds are that won't

---

Shell for Problem Statement (PS)

As of _____ (date), the _____ (metric) in the
_____ (location) has [increased / decreased] from _____
(metric or %) to _____ (metric or %) and the goal was _____
(metric or %).

---

happen immediately, so you will likely need to have conversations where
either you discuss with one of the dissenting stakeholders or, even better,
you bring the two dissenting stakeholders together and ask them to help
you finalize the PS. Key point here: if you don't have consensus on the PS,
don't spend a ton of time on the DO. The desired outcome has to mirror
the problem statement, so if you edit one, you'll need to edit the other.

Building the DO is the same exercise as the PS. The only difference is
you change the shell (listed above) from "As of" to "By" and you change
the "has" before increased/decreased to "will." It's that simple.

PROBLEM STATEMENT	DESIRED OUTCOME
From 1/1 to 2/15, sales from new customers buying our red product in Seattle has dropped from 90 units per week to 70 (goal is 80).	By 5/1, sales of new customers buying our red products will increase from 70 units per week to 90 units per week (goal is 80).
Between 1/1 and 5/1 customer contact rate for online domestic orders of blue products increased from 7% to 12% (goal is 13%).	The customer contact rate for online domestic orders of blue products will decrease from 12% to 10% by 6/1 and 8% by 7/1 (goal is 13%).
For all of Q1 2012, the average revenue per customer who buys multiple orange products in the California region has doubled from $50 to $100 (goal is $64).	By end of Q2 2012, the average revenue per customer who buys multiple orange products in the California region will remain $100 (goal is $64).

Above are three examples of PS/DOs. Note the following elements of
why they are strong:

- The PS and DO are apples to apples—they both talk about the exact same bull's-eye.

- The focus is a bull's-eye in one sentence.

- The elements of the shell are there but they don't have to be in the same order.

- #1 has the two errors corrected in the PS: (1) the date is hooked to an actual date and (2) the count being assessed also has the goal mentioned.

- #2 has a real problem that is now defined in the PS and it no longer mentions the training element or the three products that were rolled out.

- #3 is actually a good problem to have but it's an unexplained problem, meaning leadership doesn't know why it happened.

- The metric for #1 is count, #2 is percentage, and #3 is dollars.

Laser Focus as a Reinvention Strategy

Most organizations need to enact such a strategy to diversify their customer base and their product lines. Remember Starbucks from earlier in the book? This is a critical step for any organization, for-profit or nonprofit. It includes analyzing where their dollars come from so that in times of economic recessions, shifts in customer preferences, or even marketing campaigns that shift the spending patterns, an organization isn't doomed. Leadership defines organizational and project focus. This is the what. Leadership also defines the people and process focus—the who and the how. Self-aware leaders know why they define the focus, whether it is an organization, product line, or project. The following are two mini cases that allow you to see this precision in action.

Nintendo Exercising Focus in Action

The gaming industry has been on fire for the last five years. With consoles seeing severe competition by online gaming, growth has been slowed by the economic downturn but not halted. Spending on hardware alone grew over $10 billion from 2010 to 2011. Gartner, a technology research company, predicts that game-related spending will reach $112 billion by 2015. Nintendo is the largest player in this industry and the product launch of their Wii product line saw 12 straight quarters of growth from 2006 to 2009.

Sure, the story of profitable growth was impressive here, but what was even more impressive was the decision-making that led to the definition of product specs for the Wii. When most competitors were spending product development dollars on next generation graphics, Nintendo used a very different tactic to win market share; they built a mental model that eliminated any dependencies on existing assumptions and reinvented how they would compete. They shifted their hardware, not their software. The result was a wand that responded to motion control. It was attractive to kids and seniors alike. And when the product team decided not to add stellar graphics, the end product was introduced for half of the price of the Wii's competition.

Here's the lesson: know exactly what you want to accomplish. Nintendo could have followed suit and tried to compete only on graphics. Or they could have introduced the wand with advanced graphics for a price point similar to their competitors. They didn't. They defined a laser focus and created two opportunities: (1) to be first to market, and (2) to have unique product differentiation. They intentionally were not trying to be all things to all people, and it worked beautifully—for a few years.

But, in 2011, year over year sales for Nintendo dropped 50 percent. The ride was strong but short-lived because of Nintendo's lack of commitment to reinvent the Wii again. Competitors expanded the shelf life of wand-based gaming but they also incorporated advanced graphic interfaces. Nintendo's lead in this niche market was overrun by their competitors.

Taking on the High School Dropout Crisis

City Year is a well-established nonprofit that is focused on helping kids do better in school. For years, almost 2,000 17-24 year-old youths each year dressed in red jackets and Timberland boots and worked in schools across the globe to help teachers and students achieve greater academic success. Founded by two Harvard graduates, City Year adds resources in the form of young adults who would tutor, support, and role model in high-need public schools. City Year commits to making a difference in the lives of the teachers, students, and classrooms they serve. They measured everything, and while that served them well in early years, the data that detailed their past was about to reinvent their future.

In 2005, City Year had a presence in 10 sites across the United States and one in South Africa. They were approaching their 20th anniversary and their staff was loyal, their corps was excited, and their mission was good but somewhat general. Over the years, their resources had led to a wide variety of service projects, from academic to environmental and everything in between. A constant had been a truly contagious aura about City Year—they led with the heart of a nonprofit and the mind of a for-profit. They had all the numbers to keep score, but it wasn't until they shifted their focus that they pinpointed what game they were playing.

Several points led City Year to this shift. First, the Pew Partnership for Civic Change had produced a report entitled *The High School Dropout Crisis* that indicated 1/3 of all high school students in the United States don't graduate. Further, a report, *Locating the Dropout Crisis*, found that half of all dropouts are concentrated in 15 percent of the schools. Finally, Dr. Robert Balfanz further went on to define that there are three early indicators as to whether or not students are at risk of dropping out—the ABC model—attendance, behavior, and proficiency in core curriculum. Furthermore, the study showed that presence of these indicators can be detected as early as the sixth grade and in high poverty environments, and up to 75 percent of sixth- to ninth-grade students with even one offtrack indicator do not graduate high school.

By 2009, City Year had tripled their applications for young adults that want to do a year of service. They had increased the number of corps members that commit to a second year of service. They had grown their funding from corporate foundations. But no outcome was greater than clarifying their focus. They no longer would strive to have a presence in as many urban schools as they could. They would strive to have a presence in the schools that needed the most help—those with the highest dropout rates. This very intentional shift changed everything. The spirit, purpose, and discipline of City Year was no longer just about

The Starfish Story, by City Year

A young girl was walking along a beach upon which thousands of starfish had been washed up during a terrible storm. When she came to each starfish, she would pick it up, and throw it back into the ocean. People watched her with amusement.

She had been doing this for some time when a man approached her and said, "Little girl, why are you doing this? Look at this beach! You can't save all these starfish. You can't begin to make a difference!"

The girl seemed crushed, suddenly deflated. But after a few moments, she bent down, picked up another starfish, and hurled it as far as she could into the ocean. Then she looked up at the man and replied,

"Well, I made a difference to that one!"

The old man looked at the girl inquisitively and thought about what she had done and said. Inspired, he joined the little girl in throwing starfish back into the sea. Soon others joined, and all the starfish were saved.

—adapted from *The Star Thrower* by Loren C. Eiseley

the student that needed help, it was about the right intervention for the right students at the right time.

City Year now knows the address of the schools they want to work with the most. They now can partner with other organizations to look at the full life cycle of the student and not just focus on their time in high school. They can work with teachers to directly influence the students most at risk of dropping out.

Prior to the plan, people connected with City Year because the passion was there for upgrading education. Today people connect with City Year because they see the path to educational reform. Staff, volunteers, board members, and sponsors are all more focused and more committed because they know exactly who the competition is and exactly how to win.

Chapter Summary

Everyone is hungry and everyone wants to be fed. Leadership requires the self-awareness to prioritize who is the most important group to feed. They understand how long food will last and how the nourishment will change the productivity of those fed. You can feed someone with resources or information or plenty of other things, but if you don't stop to truly pinpoint your focus, you may not be feeding the right family with the right food.

Self-aware leaders who feed a family versus solve world hunger specifically:

1. Define the root of a problem. Leaders must go beyond the correct target and define the right bull's-eye, something much more precise than a common target.

2. Build one-sentence problem statements and desired outcomes for their stakeholders to agree upon as the focus.

3. Pinpoint the focus by using data. This data could come in the form of discussions, reports, or surveys.

There is risk in pinpointing the focus, but there is also a greater likelihood for success. The key to mitigating your risk is involving others. As you build your problem statement and desired outcome, validate your approach not only with data, but also with the others who will be affected by this change. Leverage others to set you up for success, not slow you down.

Chapter Nine

WHO YOU KNOW AND WHO KNOWS YOU

"Call it a clan, call it a network, call it a tribe, call it a family; whatever you call it, whoever you are, you need one."

—Elizabeth Jane Howard, English novelist

People. People who need people. Yes, Barbra Streisand was actually on to something. If you want to lead, you need people to follow. Thus leadership is a very, very relationship-driven business. So how strong is your reception with your network? No different than the smartphone on your hip, you can walk around and your reception changes based on your surroundings. Sometimes you have all five bars and sometimes you have no service. This affects your ability to send and receive messages, your ability to have a voice and be heard, and your ability to lead. This chapter will speak to the purpose and power of a professional network and support system. It will help readers define what they want from it and then who they need in it. Your network is defined as the relationships you possess to help you accomplish your goals. These relationships only go as deep as necessary, never further. Your support system, however, is a subset of your network with a deeper relationship that mutually benefits both parties.

Ten Thousand Cups of Coffee

In *Outliers*, Malcolm Gladwell quantifies that the minimum number of hours needed to achieve mastery of a skill is 10,000. Most people consider this 10,000 hours as a bar for mastery of a technical skill like playing hockey, programming computers, or managing projects. But this mark is also appropriate for less tangible, more theoretical tasks. It takes 10,000 hours to master mahjong on your iPhone, and it takes 10,000 hours to master serving on the board of a nonprofit. So, does it take 10,000 hours to be a more effective leader? Probably, but Gladwell's theory may be even more specific than this. What if Gladwell told you to strive for 10,000 hours of networking?

Over time, you will come across many patterns. The patterns could be of who wants to meet with you and who doesn't. Or the patterns could also be of what they want to talk about and what they don't. Self-aware leaders recognize the stories behind the patterns. They pay enough attention to the frequency and the message of each individual instance and build a way to leverage the aggregate information—no different than any other means of market research.

The path to 10,000 hours of networking is shorter than you think. Most leaders just have to break some habits. Resist paying too much attention to work friendships that place you in a comfort zone. Schedule time with others. Talk shop over a cup of coffee. Walk over to another office or cubicle rather than just sending an email.

The leader who stays at her desk through lunch time may think she is being more productive. She may think she is doing her organization a service. But anything that keeps a leader away from other people may prove unproductive in the long run. It certainly keeps us from completing our 10,000 hours.

Peter Drucker, the man who many claim invented the study of management, once said, "More business decisions occur over lunch and dinner than at any other time, yet no MBA courses are given on the subject." Strong networkers know people are a means to an end, but they also know to never treat people as merely a means to an end. Truly knowing people, caring for them genuinely, and studying them is the key to organizational leadership. After all, an organization's work is done by people and for people. Leaders who get work done through others will outproduce those who depend on themselves. These leaders know to communicate their goals and strengths. They are self-aware, so their awareness of others brings organizational value.

Numbers Help, But Trust Works Better

Numbers influence a leader's ability to reinvent, but make no mistake, it's not about the size of your LinkedIn network or your number of Facebook friends. How many of your Twitter followers would actually, well, follow you? Viable networks are much more than popularity contests. They are filled with trusted followers who would go to bat for you without hesitation. Pull together the right list of followers, and your network could be your most valuable asset. Think about the leaders in your organization who have the most success. Do they know the right people? Do the right people like them? Do you think that just happened accidentally?

But this is not exclusively about how many people you know. It's also about how many people know you. Over time, as you grow your career, you also have the chance to grow your network. The operative word is chance. So many otherwise capable high potentials ignore the opportunity. They reserve networking for conferences and cocktail parties, but they do not put the hours in as a daily part of their leadership brand. Part of this misconception comes from the fact that too many leaders see networking as a means to one particular end: finding their next job. Self-aware leaders recognize that a strong network breeds success today, in their current job, as well as tomorrow in their next.

A network's strength has very little to do with the job titles or big names it contains. This network might look impressive when scrolling through

Online Networking

The teenagers who crowned Facebook the king of all media are now your direct reports. They use Facebook and Twitter to cultivate social contacts and grow your business, but the research is showing that they struggle with rapport and interpersonal skills. These Millennials will make up half the workforce by 2020. They are able to mobilize large groups of virtual contacts through savvy social networking skills. Yet they'll probably underwhelm at a breakfast roundtable. The face of networking will continue to evolve. That may inspire you but it may intimidate you. But while one thousand Facebook friends, or real-life ones for that matter, does not make a leader, one Tweet can explode or derail a leader's momentum. Self-aware leaders pay attention to patterns—patterns they understand and patterns they don't. It's an ongoing effort to stay in the know.

a BlackBerry, but what could it be worth if the leader can't actually call on any of these people? Networks only grow in value when they are chocked with trusted colleagues. And you can only build a network of trusted colleagues one way. Be a trusted colleague. Be humble with your title and selfless with your time. Each relationship in your contact list must show substance, not name flashing. It should be filled with people who share your desire to reinvent. People who want to help you because you have helped or will help them. Business cards collected with no solid connection are useless. They are no different than initiating a cold call for life insurance—you'll need 10 no's to get a yes.

Leaders need to develop a perspective on the importance of numbers as it relates to the reinvention process. Chapter 1 highlighted research on high potential leaders who lack the ability and confidence to use numbers effectively by delegating work. Delegation flaws are basically thinly-veiled trust issues. It may not be that the non-delegating leader doesn't trust his reports. It's probably that he doesn't trust that the report will do the work the way he wants it done. This lack of trust blurs the line between leadership and control. Control freaks covet their work; they want to own everything about it. Self-aware leaders delegate with trust. That is how they grow their numbers. They get work done by utilizing the strengths of others and leading them to project completion. Team members are then successful and also grow to trust their leader. The system feeds itself.

How 9/11 Changed Trust in the Workplace

In 2009 the *Harvard Business Review* summer cover story was all about trust. The world was facing a massive recession and organizational cutbacks were increasing unemployment. But the tragedies of 9/11 changed how trust influences the workplace in two ways. First, it further polarized employee/employer loyalty as the economic tailspin highlighted that bad things can happen to good people. Second, there was a movement in goodness—volunteerism levels skyrocketed and feel-good stories started to permeate the normal readout of homicides on the six o'clock news. People had found time to be good again. The world has morphed from a culture that values creation, to one that values collaboration, and now it's being called participation. If people trust you, they will give you the time of day; and if they don't, they will give you the cold shoulder. The big question is whether trust in goodness is greater than fear of bad things happening to good people.

Imagine a snowball rolling down a hill. Think of the snowball as your aggregate network and support system. Let's say the snowball at the top of the hill is six inches in diameter and (for round number's sake) therefore consists of 6,000 snowflakes. If you look around the hill, you'll likely see snowballs that are bigger and smaller than yours. To be more successful—to be a better leader—you wonder, "Shouldn't my snowball be bigger?" On one hand, biggest isn't always best. Huge snowballs are hard to manage. On the other hand, bigger snowballs generate more momentum and are therefore more difficult to stop.

It's not the size of your network; it's how you use it. Instead of worrying about size, learn the difference between a contact and a connection. This creates the bridge between acquiring a network and converting that network into a support system. They are not mutually exclusive. You can have an individual in your network that is not in your support system, and you can have someone who is in both. The important part is that you recognize that (a) there are two populations and (b) influence comes from leaders who leverage both.

Networking is about the stickiness of connections that help propel a leader's overall productivity and therefore, their career. It's not just who you know, it's also how quickly you can access your connections. Also, it's important to know how far they are willing to go for you. If you have a strong network and support system at your fingertips, if they trust you and you trust them, then your ability to compete will be stronger than others around you.

Analyze What vs. Who You Can Access

Self-awareness is built from learning through reflection. Self-aware leadership takes that reflection and upgrades it into action. This next exercise is an opportunity for you to do both. Part one asks you to answer a series of questions to further analyze the breadth and depth of your network. Part two then builds off this exercise by tasking you with analyzing the people you consider the strongest connections in your network.

Part 1: What Do You Have Access to?

Below is a series of questions that identify how quickly you can access certain information points from your existing network. Indicate "Y" for yes if you do have someone in your network with this formation, and "N" for no if you don't. If you indicate "Y," list the initials of the person in your network you can leverage for this information.

PROFESSIONAL	Y	N	PERSONAL	Y	N
Someone with firsthand experience in mergers and acquisitions.			Someone who knows about the logistics of getting kids accepted into college.		
Someone who could get you a job interview at a top employer in your city.			Someone who could give advice on running a marathon.		
Someone who has a tremendous financial mind to help you assess a business plan.			Someone who could talk you through what it is like to live with cancer.		

PROFESSIONAL	Y	N	PERSONAL	Y	N
Someone who had to shut down a business or part of a business.			Someone who could help you start your own nonprofit.		
Someone who could introduce you to a peer in another city you are considering moving to.			Someone who could assess if you are receiving good legal advice.		
Someone who could get you 10 minutes with a specific senior executive on an idea you have.			Someone who could talk you through how to prioritize your home repairs for resell value.		
Someone who has worked for a business that went bankrupt.			Someone who could get you invited to a very exclusive social event.		
Someone who ran a million dollar plus sales organization.			Someone that has converted religions.		
Someone who has worked in both nonprofit and for-profit.			Someone who has recent military experience.		

So as you review the list, what is your reaction? Did you have more than you thought? Do the areas where you have connections missing have anything in common? Look at the items you selected yes for your answer. How many of those people could you get 30 minutes with in the next week? This starts to define how strong your connections are. It also helps you identify gaps. If you use this insight to forecast the network and support system you will need in the future based on career goals, project goals, or personal goals, you can start building that network and support system now. This takes time and patience—and trust. And all of it must be intentional on what you have in your network and support system plus what you need.

Part 2: Who Do You Have Access to?

In her book *Working Identity*, Herminia Ibarra drives home a very interesting point around this. She provides a very valuable lesson in managing your network that is closely tied to brand. If you rely on your existing network to help you make a transformative change in your career, you will be limited. People will see you and label you as the professional that you were, not what you want to be. They have you in a box. Ibarra suggests building a network outside your normal network that doesn't already see you in that box. The definition of insanity is often stated as doing the same thing over and over and expecting different results. Ibarra's version: Using the same network over and over again and expecting a different response. You have to always go after new and different snowflakes to allow you to expand your network in new and different ways. If you want to drive substantive change with your next move, you may consider leaning on people you don't generally lean on.

If you think about the 20 most valuable individuals in your network, what exactly is their value? If you follow Ibarra's logic, are they giving you more than you already have, or just more of the same? This exercise is meant to question the assumptions you have about your existing network. Sure, you know them. Sure, they feel comfortable. Sure, they will respond to you. But is that enough?

Building a network is an intentional exercise. If all of management boils down to tasks and people, then what happens if you analyze your network the same way? On the one hand you have a list of people that you can go to for something specific. Your lead in is the task at hand. On the other hand you have people you can go to for anything. They'd step in front of a train from you regardless of what kind of train it is. Self-aware leaders are intentional about (a) having two lists and (b) knowing who they have and who they want on each list.

Task Based Connections →	What You Have Access To	← People Based Connections

Relationships are hard work. You have to invest time to build rapport. You have to open yourself to being vulnerable in order to build trust. It doesn't matter whether these connections are professional or personal. Meetings over coffee can be worth every penny if their focus is defined and intentional. Take the time to develop rapport and trust with key colleagues, and you will reap a steady network filled with people you've invested in, and who will invest in you. Though it will take time and effort, it'll also say a lot about you as a leader. Self-aware leaders know work gets done by people and for people, so they invest their time in the people and not just the work.

Six Tips on Growing Your Network

Self-aware leaders actively grow their networks. Below are six best practices for increasing yours. They are listed in no particular order.

Be authentically interested and humble.

No one likes to build a new relationship with someone who is full of himself. Relationships are a two-way street, so if you want to build trust, you need to care about the other person. If the only time you contact them is when you need something, then you don't really care—or at least your actions are not showing that you care.

Target a list of well-networked people you don't know.

Be intentional in targeting candidates for your network. Identify a social opportunity to connect and use that as an instrument for an introduction. Work at rapport development. When you go to a dinner, meet people you don't know. Network and sit with people one "level" above you, but do it in a way that humbly positions you as a colleague and not as a kiss-up. To do this you must (a) not be starstruck by them, (b) create safe dialogue that doesn't position you as taking advantage of their influence and (c) build a connection around something other than their most powerful card. There will be no handouts from your network but doors will be opened by them.

As much as possible, meet in their office.

Visibility comes from different things: success in your work, being vocal on key issues, and being seen with others outside of your office. A key tactic in growing your network is getting away from your home court. A teenage ball player who wants to be recognized for his basketball skills will always be considered soft until he wins some games in other neighborhoods. Go to someone else's home court and win. It shows more than skills; it shows heart. As you schedule out your project meetings, stay away from your home court so you can subtly increase your visibility. You never know who you'll meet when you are out there.

Network to create value, not to get a job.

This is one of the most significant points to be made about networking. If the only reason you network and the only time you network is when you need a job, people will see right through you. Think of networking like building an election campaign. You have to have an election date in your mind. It may be three months from now or three years from now. But if the first time you meet someone you ask, "Do I have your vote?" you will turn them off because they know nothing about you. It takes time to position yourself and by the way, people who network to create value in the work they do today generally don't have to network for jobs—people come to them because they already know their value.

Probe with questions more than you tell your own story.

Basketball great Charles Barkley once said, "You can talk without saying a thing. I don't ever want to be that type of person." There's a reason Sir Charles doesn't run a call center. Developing a network fit for reinvention is asking more than you tell. Everyone knows that listening is the more important side of basic communication; it's just that no one listens to that advice. Ask a lot of questions when networking. Not only is this the fastest path out of small talk and into meaningful exchanges, but it also leads toward uncovering a person's goals, strengths, and passions. These areas are important for effective networking and will often allow for common ground or future collaboration. Questions show that you care. They disarm people. They encourage interesting stories that truly reveal a person's inner self. They can also help you more quickly identify a person who may ultimately turn you off. Besides, everyone loves talking about themselves. Providing an outlet for people to talk about themselves will make you a very necessary part of *their* network.

Send a handwritten thank you note on your personal stationery.

How many emails have you received in the last week? OK, got the number? Now how many handwritten thank you notes have you received in the last week? Not even close, is it? If you want to be remembered, you have to do things that others aren't doing. Not so you make yourself look better than them, just so you are remembered. Thank you notes should be authentic and specifically state why you are grateful. It's not just a simple "thanks for buying me a cup of coffee" note. It's a "here's what I learned from you and here's why I am grateful" note.

Networks, Support Systems, and Reinvention

Reinventing, like everything else in life, requires strong and consistent positive reinforcement. It is rare that you can do it yourself. Having a support system allows you to maintain as much momentum in the lows as you have in your highs. Think about the purpose of any support group—from Alcoholics Anonymous to Weight Watchers, from industry councils to investment groups. The power is in the numbers because when you hit a roadblock or second-guess yourself, you have others on the team pushing you forward.

If you think your network is strong enough for today, then your complacency likely labels you as average. If you are building your network for paths you might need to access in the next three years, then you have moved into above average. This is what will drive your self-awareness.

Chris was a manager of operations from central Pennsylvania when he attended the Comcast high potential leadership program. Throughout the course of the year he learned many things about himself. He learned about delegation and process improvement. He learned about where the business was heading and how he fit into that vision. But it wasn't until the actual last day of the program that he learned for himself what his greatest takeaway would be. In his feedback form he wrote: "Before I entered this program I thought my job was to come into work, put my head down, and work as hard as I could. I now realize that is not enough. You can get so much more done if you get out from behind your desk and interact with others to get things done."

What if every day was an interview? Would that inspire you, influence you, or freak you out? A few years ago, it freaked Chris out. Today it influences how he leads himself and how he leads others. This increase in self-awareness was a critical piece of his reinvention and has presented him with two promotions since graduating the leadership program just a few years ago.

Chapter Summary

Self-aware leaders don't depend exclusively on themselves to feed their self-awareness. By leveraging a strong network and support system, self-aware leaders can grow themselves by growing their network. This is not about a popularity contest. Networks reciprocate on their value proposition and accentuate trust as the foundation of the connections.

More specifically, self-aware leaders leverage their network to help them reinvent self, others, and the business. Specific tactics highlighted in this chapter include:

- Start by defining what you have in your network so you will know what you need.

- Be intentional with steps that you take to grow your network, recognizing that quality connections can oftentimes trump the quantity of connections.

- Recognize that your network and support system do overlap. Trust is a key variable that allows someone to move from the former to the latter.

- Networking is not just about getting an interview or a job. Self-aware leaders proactively build their networks to help them be successful today in their work.

Chapter Ten

CONNECT THE DOTS AND SPUR INNOVATION

"Invisible threads are the strongest ties."

—Friedrich Nietzsche, 19th century German philosopher

This final chapter teaches the practice of connecting the dots, why it's important, and how to implement it. Connecting the dots is about relating seemingly unrelated items to create exponential synergy. But it's much more than one plus one equals three. The math is the science of synergy. Connecting the dots is the art. Good leaders follow the science of leadership, great leaders create art. This chapter also culminates your journey through this study of increased self-awareness. As you read these last few pages, connect the dots back to previous points made throughout the book. How does this relate to thinking like a GM? What about professional authenticity or reinventing others? It all ties together. Connect the dots helps you to apply this book's story to your story.

The History of Connecting the Dots

The first time you hear the phrase "connect-the-dots," you probably think of a five-year-old with an oversized pencil slowly tracing the outline of a clown in an activity workbook. The exercise is very linear and teaches control of the pencil and following directions.

But leadership is not simple. It is not linear. And it certainly isn't predictable. The responsibility for leading people and managing work does not come with step-by-step directions. That's the challenge of it, the pain of it, and the fun of it. It's also why some leaders are successful while others are not.

Corporate philanthropy is a perfect example of connecting the dots. Most major corporations have foundations that fund very deserving causes. These causes are not only socially deserving but are also business relevant. No one would debate that giving back is a good thing, but good causes become the right causes when the social impact involves customers. After all, customers incorporate corporate citizenship into their decisions. It is also how customers develop brand loyalty and employer loyalty. Great business leaders connect the dots between what is "good for the business" and what is good for the community and the customer.

Yet, if you leverage the above perspective on connect-the-dots and apply it to leadership, the result is somewhat similar to what Thomas Friedman was implying in his best seller *The World is Flat*. If all organizations are systems then everything is connected. The challenge is that this may not be obvious for you. Connecting the dots tasks leaders with seeing relationships that are not obvious and that others are not seeing. Leveraging profitable imagination as well as critical and systems thinking, self-aware leaders slow themselves down to visualize, list, and debate:

1. What is the current situation being assessed?
   Note: this could be a positive opportunity or a negative problem.

2. What exists outside this situation that, to an extent, mirrors or influences the situation?
   Note: this could be inside or outside your organization.

3. What can you leverage from the outside data points to better the current situation?

Note: this could be very obvious or not so much.

Think of high school biology. You learned about how things like your respiratory systems influence your circulatory and nervous systems. Each are individual systems with multiple moving parts but each also influences the productivity of the other systems. Like with our bodies, in our work we rarely slow down to think about the thousands of moving parts and pieces that fire simultaneously to make our systems move. Without knowledge of them, we can operate but we cannot truly understand. If something malfunctioned, would you know how to fix it?

That's the question you have for your business and your team—do you want to operate it, understand it, or both? You cannot simply hit the gas and expect to always excel. Everyone knows that marketing affects sales and that product development affects customer service, but identifying which connections are key to focus on is not an easy skill. Connecting the dots allows an outside perspective to create learning from data points. These data points are the dots. They serve as a foundation to create a business case for reinvention.

More Thoughts on Patterns

In the last few chapters, you've read a good deal about patterns. Patterns become powerful when you string them together—when you connect the dots. It's based on the premise that leadership is clearly part finance and economics, but it is also part psychology and sociology.

Reinventing Leadership

The first model you were introduced to in this book was the reinvention triangle. A triangle is obviously the connection of three separate elements. The simplicity of the model is the convenience and attractiveness of these connected dots. But the complexity of the model, how the three reinventions interact, and how the four pillars are grounded in self-awareness is what makes this model so powerful.

Bob Keidel, PhD, a professor at Drexel University, wrote the book, *Seeing Organizational Patterns*, which teaches a model on organizational cognition. The model articulates the complexity and power of connecting the dots by introducing four progressive levels used to observe these patterns.

The reinvention model thrives off the brilliance of Keidel's triangular concept. The reinvention model is as clean and memorable as the point pattern, but it's multifaceted enough to be complex in its application to any organization, individual, or instance. The interdependence that the triangular pattern presents is what gives this reinvention model versatility. For example, this model can be used as a proactive planning tool as well as a retrospective analysis tool. It can be used by a young whippersnapper five years out of his MBA or by a long-time veteran looking to transition into semi-retirement. The pronounced relationship between the three points drives the fact that all three areas of reinvention (self, others, and the business) must be present to make the model work. The complexity lies in using judgment to identify the level of emphasis on which each situation is based.

Keidel's Model

1. <u>Point</u> = seeing only one moment in time

2. <u>Linear</u> = seeing a beginning and an end

3. <u>Angular</u> = the first time one starts to see the relationship between two things as creating a win-win relationship

4. <u>Triangular</u> = one sees the complexity and interdependence of relationships from a three-dimensional perspective

—Bob Keidel, *The Geometry of Strategy* (Routledge 2010).

Seeing the Connections

In this competitive world where middle managers are so strong at the *get 'er done* approach, a flaw exists. The flaw is based on a leader's need to quickly solve the issue at hand and not get bogged down. After all, there are 37 other issues that are waiting in the queue for that leader's attention, so they need speed to close the deal and check it off the list.

One of the best methods for organizationally visualizing connecting the dots is an exercise called mapping. Before explaining how mapping works, think about maps as they pertain to driving from one location to another. The world, for so many years, depended on maps. If you're over 35 years old, in your glove compartment or trunk, you likely had an atlas or fold-up map. You got it from AAA or a life insurance agent. The world has now transformed into being much more transactional. Speed matters. Decisions need to be made quickly and with minimal distraction. Information is only as practical as it is convenient. Enter the GPS. You don't need to read the map. The GPS will read the map and explain it to you. The GPS is prescriptive, and it supposedly takes all of the guesswork out of navigation.

Leadership is not prescriptive. It is not like a GPS. It requires analysis. It needs to be read and deciphered. And that's what high potential leaders are attracted to. They want to be the voice on the GPS, not the driver listening carefully. High potentials dream of being navigators. They want to fix it, finish it, and move on to the next challenge. Self-aware leaders know that you can't actually learn about where you are going from a GPS. They know that depending on the GPS means never knowing where they're going. So they read the maps. They account for much more than the start point and the end point. They do this in project decisions and even career decisions.

There are several types of maps you can use:

Mind maps allow you to brainstorm in a way that organizes. Mind maps rely on the creation of multidimensional figures to represent data instead of a one dimensional organizational device like a list or a note. In other words, mind-mapping experts preach the importance of creating visual representations of information, data, and basically anything that needs to be digested or learned. The thinking is that these objects, like shapes or graphics, are more easily integrated into groups or sequences so that dot connection is more intuitive and easier.

Collision maps let you play the role of air traffic controller. You may not be flying all the planes, but you do have the insight and data to analyze what will hit whom and when. An example of this might be a swim lane diagram that defines by launch date all the different communication that will change your employee base. You can see if you have too many hit at once. The visual of these collisions really helps intensify focus and global thinking. If you've ever had an accident or near accident, think about how much you pay attention immediately after it happens. Your focus is stronger and that focus gives you self-awareness.

Heat maps indicate differences in data by colors and clustering (another word for patterns). Web heat maps are the easiest example to visualize this model. For example, if you wanted to examine the data of which aspects of a website are most often visited, a heat map would help by glowing the high traffic points.

Weather maps inform you to use science and data for your predictions. Instead of looking at metrics like temperature, humidity, and barometric pressure, this type of weather map examines metrics critical to your business. Power companies use weather maps to analyze consumption. Consider blackouts. Many times they were due to the fact that an accurate monitoring system was not in place to anticipate demand being greater than supply. Power outages significantly affect a company's brand, revenue, and customer service. If they saw them coming, these risks could have been minimized.

This book is not designed to sell a particular mapping style. The above is meant to encourage you to try one, or all, on for size. Once you find the one or ones that work (and the appropriate situations for each), use them regularly. Self-aware leaders are challenged on a daily basis to execute. And yet if that's all they do, they will live a full life, but only full of execution. Self-aware leaders pick their heads up and look beyond the turn-by-turn directions. They see what else is going on in the neighborhoods they are driving through. They analyze windshield time versus productivity time. They take control of the wheel.

Brian's Real Life Collision

Those who are truly savvy at organizational politics plot out collision maps. Because in business it's never just about the project; it's about the projects. Anyone can implement a single project but how that complements or interferes with other projects is what makes things complex—visually mapping which key projects literally affect one another in terms of timing, bandwidth, and other factors.

Brian led a team of 10 training professionals. He called a meeting with five of his peers who were all working on separate projects leading separate functional teams—human resources, customer service, and so forth. He started this meeting with a blank whiteboard, but ended it with consensus that there was a problem. The tool he used was a collision map using swim lanes.

In one hour he took each of the five separate initiatives and plotted out major milestones. As the third, fourth, and fifth projects were plotted onto the timeline, lightbulbs began sparking around the room. The other four executives were so focused on their individually functional projects that they were ignoring the projects taking off and landing on other runways. Brian's collision map taught others how to connect the dots. Seventy percent of all learning is visual, and this map plotted exactly where the different runaway planes would collide in midair.

The most effective part of Brian and his collision map was his communication method. He needed to "say" something, but couldn't come right out and say it. So, Brian used the other voices in the room. By asking the right questions, being patient with the process, and leveraging the individual areas present at the meeting, Brian was able to achieve his intended outcome without rattling egos, challenging sensibilities, or ruffling feathers. Instead, he simply led participants down the road to a solution. Instead of becoming combative against his ideas, they solved the problem for him.

Applying Connecting the Dots
in Your Organization

So how does connecting the dots apply to your organization? Think about the following three questions:

- What does a marketing campaign have to do with employee retention?

- What does management's commitment to the community say about brand loyalty?

- How does investing in the customer experience positively affect profitability?

Many mature organizations have leaders who have mastered the art of connecting the dots. They exist specifically as a conduit between "good" and "right." They serve a role that aligns and appropriately sequences organizational initiatives. In most businesses, how things get done inspires success far more greatly than what gets done. The reality is that leaders who connect the dots always think globally about the ripple effect of decisions. Leaders who connect the dots not only see the proverbial forest for the trees, but they also initiate a plan to conserve and protect that forest, while not forgetting to publish a few press releases along the way.

The question is whether you see these connections proactively or reactively. Proactive connecting of the dots is leadership; reactive is management. . . and in some cases, crisis management. For several years, Comcast had great success in teaching this connect-the-dots theory to our leaders. The rationale was based on Comcast's product evolution. At the time of the new millennium, Comcast had only two core products: a fairly substantive video business and a relatively new Internet product. The businesses were run separately via different technical teams and different areas in the call center; the two worlds were sequestered from one another. Leaders could be successful within their own function exclusively, yet still be considered high potential.

That all changed once Comcast launched a third product: Voice. The "triple play" not only changed things for the customer, but also for our

Connecting the Dots in College Basketball

Joe Lunardi's extraordinary career success is a story rooted in self-awareness. As the inventor of a unique methodology for figuring out the likely top contenders in the National Collegiate Association of America (NCAA) playoffs, Joe has literally changed the face of college basketball; and he did it by simply following the call of his passion—basketball.

It all began in the early 1990s when Joe developed a widely-followed publication that carefully analyzed the top 100 teams in the NCAA. Joe spent untold hours putting this publication together in addition to holding down his job as the vice president of communications for Saint Joseph's University (SJU). Joe's analysis was dead accurate; he was picking the teams in March Madness with utter precision. As a fan base grew, Joe saw an opportunity. He didn't want to become rich and retire early. He just wanted to be an important figure in this game he loved.

Over time, Joe's team rating methodology matured and eventually acquired the name bracketology. At the time, Joe couldn't have known that he was reinventing college basketball scheduling. Instead of hoarding the math that he had created to make his predictions, Joe shared the science behind it. Soon, sports broadcasting giant ESPN would come calling. ESPN adopted Joe's bracketology system and marketed it to millions of sports fans. Today, journalists, sports broadcasters, and even coaches and athletic directors live and die by Joe's predictions.

Today, Joe still works for SJU; however, he has had an unimaginable impact on the game he loves. Joe's self-awareness guided his journey from the beginning. He knew what he wanted to do, and he followed his passion wherever it took him. More importantly, he has enjoyed every day of the ride.

Joe's story is a good example of where self-awareness can take an individual or a leader. The story also illustrates that growing your self-awareness is not just about helping you climb a corporate ladder to a specific level of success. Joe's transparent approach ended up being the catalyst for his growth. The ultimate goal of self-awareness, as discussed in this book, is to help you build your own brand through self-awareness; and this enlightenment in turn will enable you to climb any ladder you choose to climb.

leaders and employees. Cross-functional success became pivotal to our business. Comcast intended to blur our separate products into a single package, so the same integration needed to exist in Comcast's leadership.

Customers wanted to call into Comcast and deal with one person, not three. The shift was felt across the entire organization. Comcast University was now tasked with developing general managers, regardless of their role or function. The challenge was for all leaders to think, analyze, and act like general managers regardless of whether their title said director of customer service, marketing, finance, or technical operations.

Today, the mantra at Comcast is *OneComcast*. It's built around working across functional business units to simplify the internal processes that drive the customer experience. It's making a difference in how our leaders scope the work, how our employees do the work, and how our customers respond to the work. And the difference is measurable and profitable.

Chapter Summary

Connecting the dots is about relating two seemingly unrelated items. This correlation allows leaders a new path to creating value. By leveraging organizational strategies, the high potential leader can tap into a broader understanding of the ways in which her daily professional life fits into more global projections of her aspirations. Connecting the dots is about stopping to ask the right questions. How does what we do today lead us toward what we want to become? The self-aware leader knows that how we connect the dots isn't nearly as important as the fact that we commit to the process overall.

Three questions that enhance your ability to connect the dots are:

- What is the current situation being assessed?
- What exists outside this situation that, to an extent, mirrors or influences the situation?
- What can you leverage from the outside data points to better the current situation?

The value of connecting the dots is infinite. This is not a skill that you will develop overnight, but with practice and positive reinforcement of both successes and failures, you'll learn how it enriches your leadership output.

CONCLUSION

I've worked with hundreds of high potential leaders in integrating this model into their lives, to increase professional fulfillment as well as overall productivity. They embrace the model—all of it. I felt it and the research validated it. But throughout it all, my key takeaway has been that there is no one size fits all approach. Self-aware leaders know what is right and when it is right. They get it.

The Self-Aware Leader

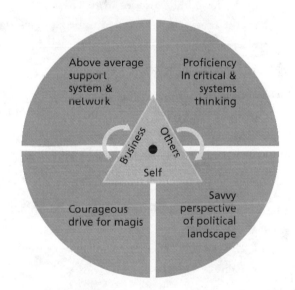

Chapter 10 taught the principles of connecting the dots as a leadership practice. The reality is that it's also a career practice. As mentioned in the earlier part of this book, the line between our personal and professional lives is fading very quickly. Self-aware leaders connect the dots between what they want out of their lives and their work.

The purpose of this conclusion is to afford you one last opportunity to reflect before you put this book down, or pass it to a colleague. Use these three sections to truly think about what you will do to propel your self-awareness. Every aspect of this book is intentional. Finish strong.

Lessons From the Plovers

If you ever vacation in Ocean City, New Jersey, you will see small, triangular tracks in the sand. Too small for seagulls, but too big for the birds inhabiting the surrounding dunes, these tracks belong to piping plovers, a nearly extinct nesting bird indigenous to the area. The plovers have a pretty rough life. Their eggs are regularly trampled by tourists or devoured by natural predators like foxes and gulls. The birds receive state protection due to their endangered status, but that doesn't always help. Conservationists have built a series of fences around the nests to ward off intruders. The fences were designed to be large enough for the plovers to penetrate, but small enough to keep beach foxes away from enjoying an egg or two for breakfast.

Plovers always stay together. They do so to be able to care for their nests properly. One stands guard while the other hunts and gathers. If they didn't learn to remain in pairs, they'd have been extinct already. The fences that interloping conservationists build around plovers are intricate devices that require many man hours to assemble correctly. Why go to all the trouble? Why not just trap the foxes? The conservationists know that protecting a nest is much better than removing a predator. It helps the species thrive. Without foxes around, the plovers would become despondent and lazy. They need the predators. It forces them to build up their nests and keep enough food.

Plovers can teach us a great deal about self-awareness, survival, and success in general. Leaders need to focus on the importance of building a strong nest around their organizations. To do this, they need to build themselves up and connect the dots among the vital success factors. Yes, foxes circle nearby, but they may help as much as they harm. If their presence reminds us to continually build and grow, then strangely, what threatens our existence is also what keeps us thriving. Oh, and by the way, it always helps to keep a buddy nearby, just in case.

Professional Patience

Your style of leadership is a very personal decision. Just like the plovers, everyone is motivated differently. Yet there are clearly some tactics that research has proven to be more effective than others. Throughout the course of reading this book, you have likely paused and asked yourself the following questions:

- How happy am I in my current job? Am I more busy or more challenged?

- Is this where I expected to be right now? Am I OK with the pace of my growth?

- How do others perceive my leadership brand?

- Do I have champions actively working networks to advance my career?

- What core values are being emphasized by my current work? De-emphasized?

As you finish this book you hopefully have more answers than questions. Sure, this type of read will play with your mind a bit, but that's the sign of a good book. It makes you think different and it makes you act different. Life happens fast. Self-aware leaders use patience when reinventing. Now is not always the time.

Let's use Phil as an example. Phil graduates from a good college and lands a good job. His immediate focus is to show his company that he adds value to his team. This sentiment is an unconscious priority of *reinvent the business*. Phil pours his essence into proving himself by building up his organization. As years pass, Phil eventually marries that cute girl from the coffee shop. In turn, Phil puts a decent amount of pressure on himself to make more money, so his wife can stay at home with their kids. Based on his successful business reinvention, Phil gets promoted, tackles more responsibility, and is now managing a team of direct reports.

After attending a leadership program, a mentor tells Phil that he's never going to get anywhere unless he builds a team that is highly productive and, to a large degree, self-sufficient. This advice awakens a change in Phil's thinking. He must focus on *reinventing others*—both at work and at home. Phil must do this in order to remain successful at work, because in his new professional role, reinventing the business requires that Phil reinvent others, namely his team. At home, Phil focuses on cultivating a successful, happy, and healthy family by focusing on others—his wife and kids. Parenting is the world's most selfless act.

Fast forward 15 years. Phil faces his first midlife crisis. His kids are in college. The nest is empty. He buys the cliché convertible. Nothing helps. So, Phil decides to shake up his career. He pursues something he has "always wanted to do." He propels himself into his work. He reinvents this new business and has tremendous success doing so. As Phil nears retirement, he realizes that he cannot use work as his sole source of accomplishment and success. He turns to giving back to his community as a big brother and a mentor to small business owners. Phil moves into full retirement and finds that he has to reinvent self to enjoy his extra time. He takes up golf and teaches at a local community college to keep himself active.

Phil has a choice every day when he wakes up. Will his life be an autobiography or a biography?

You have that same choice.

There is no correct pace to apply this model. Life gets in the way and it should. You cannot predict the curveballs life will throw at you. You can define what the right timing is for you based on what you are experiencing and what you want. Self-aware leaders set their own pace. As Henry David Thoreau stated:

> *"Go confidently in the direction you intended. Live the life you have always imagined."*

Every Ending is a New Beginning

Marcia entered this leadership program as a functional information technology expert but her leadership presence lacked. Over the course of her reinvention she learned how to have the voice of a leader, and now she mentors other women on how to find their voice.

Kevin entered this leadership program as a passionate workhorse who drove his team to hit their numbers. His reinvention taught his team how to hit their numbers and because of that, he was promoted twice.

Donya entered this leadership program as a simple leader driving for functional success at one location. Her reinvention grew her ability to think like a GM, connect the dots, and reinvent the business. This substantive shift positioned for opportunities in managing multiple markets.

Each of these individuals represents the hundreds that have entered the Comcast leadership program as one type of leader and left the program as another. The goal was not to change who they were as people. Individuality is important and there is no single leadership style at Comcast or at your organization. Reinventing maintains the soul of who you are but shifts the mechanics on how you execute. Through increased self-awareness, leaders learn how to anticipate what will drive progress and they then commit to perpetual reinvention.

Today's world will see many of the new inventions but most will be in the form of reinventions. Technology and information will drive these reinventions as upgrades to existing strategies, products, and processes. There will only be so many iPhones that revolutionize an entire industry. But leaders need to be the catalyst for rallying people around these new technologies and information points. Those leaders who can see and hear what others can't will be more successful. They know how to connect the dots by relating seemingly unrelated things.

Your Turn

If you read this book and are inspired, that's nice. It will give you a warm and fuzzy feeling inside. But if that's where it ends, you've fallen short. It's no different than attending a conference that tells you what, but not how. This book is meant to inspire a perpetual commitment to reinvention. That commitment to doing it successfully comes from stronger self-awareness and a robust support system that pushes you in a healthy way. The two combined represent a proven model for success in middle management today.

So what will you do to get the ball rolling and find momentum to fuel your reinvention? How will you increase your self-awareness so you maximize your strengths and address your weaknesses? Here are six final suggestions to put things in motion:

- Go online and find a job description for something that gives you goose bumps. It could be your next job, but an even better exercise is to find the job after that.

- Ask your manager or a mentor how far off you are from being a solid candidate for that opportunity. Then ask if it fulfills your passion to work or just your need to work.

- Identify specific knowledge, skills, and abilities that you need to collect in order for you to be the best candidate for that job.

- Prioritize those reinventions and classify them as reinventing self, others, or the business so you can be intentional with your focus.

- Project manage this no different than how you manage any other work project. Have a deadline with milestones to monitor progress. Schedule cups of coffee.

- Build your exit strategy knowing that in order for you to move out of the job you are in, you need to teach someone else to do it just as well.

None of these suggestions imply you need a new job tomorrow. They are meant to inspire you to seek out more—however you define it. Be intentional with what you want from your work. Stay true to your values and manage your professional authenticity. Be yourself, and be your best self. Commit to the process of being self-aware and take time to reflect on what that means for you—as it will change. Success comes from reinvention but intended success comes from intentional reinvention.

Appendix

TRAINING THE SELF-AWARE LEADER

The research has proven that by learning this model, high potential leaders become more self-aware, gain more political skill, aspire for magis, and make specific gains in networking and systems thinking. So how do you create a learning solution that drives a substantive shift to align with this model?

This section is meant for training professionals who want to move the needle with strong leadership development. It gives specific suggestions on how to incorporate key principles from this book into training programs, as well as several templates. You can also go to www.gallagherleadership.com or email me at dan@gallagherleadership.com for access to more training resources.

The recommendations included in this section are based on the application of the reinvention model to the Comcast University middle management high potential program referenced in the book. The class is designed for 45 participants and runs over an eight-month period with three in-person meetings. Leaders are selected for the program based on talent reviews conducted by human resources. Participants commit to six full days of in-class time plus one to two hours per week. Before travel and expenses, the program costs about $1200 per person. More than two-thirds of the graduates are promoted within 18-24 months of graduating, but the program does not guarantee a promotion. Here are some points:

Analyze aggregate 360-degree feedback data before you start the training. Data is your friend. It starts with interviews and a few focus groups to define your bull's-eye for the training program. Don't try and accomplish everything halfway; build a learning experience that fully immerses the learner in three to five key behaviors. If you've never done a card sorting exercise, learn what it is and do it to nail your focus. Have the participants complete the 360 before they start the training. This way you will know the persona of the group and how they stack up to the three to five items. Show the participants not only their individual data but also their aggregate data. Stick with the same tool for a few years and bam—you can now show the trends of the aggregate data. If you have a leadership program that operates at the next title up, use the same tool and show the difference between a director population and a vice president population. Last point: make sure that the leaders build individual development plans with partial or full focus on the three to five behaviors you have identified as central to the program. To do this well, you want to reference these behaviors every step of the program.

Over-engage managers with "just add water and stir" communications. The participant's manager has the most influence over the training program's effectiveness. Yes, the learner needs to initiate the new behavior, but the manager will be the one who reinforces or dismisses the new way of leading. If you build a multi-session learning experience, over-engage the leaders. This won't guarantee that additional conversations happen, but it will increase the likelihood. The design of your training program should include a specific focus on the role of the participant's leader. First, they should be at the orientation webinar, with their team member, to fully understand the roadmap and their role as it pertains to each step. Second, they should be supplied with probing questions to ask of their reports. They should be provided with expected outcomes and ways to gauge responses from the participant's team members. This is process accountability. Send a follow-up email to the participants and their managers. Both sides will then understand what they are supposed to talk about throughout the process. There should be no secrets or surprises. Third, schedule a call/webinar with them two days after each live training and optionally invite the participants to observe. Lastly, the managers of participants should applaud trying, succeeding, and failing with the new behaviors. As Robinson and Robinson stated in *Training for Impact*,

Learning Experience × Work Environment = Business Results,

the managers create the environment for change…or they don't. The first sample is a piece of communication that goes to all managers and participants after a live training session. The second sample is an individual scorecard that summarizes individual progress upon completion of the program.

2011 FUNDAMENTALS OF LEADERSHIP INDIVIDUAL SCORECARD	
[Insert Name, Title, Location]	
Key Result Areas	
Performance Goal as of 1/1/11: • • •	Results as of 9/1/11 • • •
360-Degree Feedback Data	
3 Strength Areas: • • •	New Behaviors/Results: • • •
3 Developmental Areas: • • •	New Behaviors/Results • • •
Community Investment Activity	
Project Summary:	Lessons Learned:
Process Improvement	
Problem Statement:	Results as of 9/1/11:
Desired Outcome:	Next Steps:
FOL Mentor:	

Build action learning projects that keep the attention of learners and executives. Action learning requires training participants to take new behaviors and models for leadership and apply them to real work environments. At Comcast, we did two different projects. The first was a service learning project. If you have ever managed volunteers, you know they are more difficult to manage than a paid direct report. If a volunteer doesn't like your leadership, they will volunteer somewhere else. But there were two other reasons why we did this project:

- Having influence. Leaders need to know how to influence others, even those who do not report to them.

- Having a life. The 360 data of Comcast high potentials reveal that they are workhorses. All work and no play, well, you know how that turns out. It's important to find balance, but overwork leads to problems at home, a loss of faith, disconnect from the community. They won't stay high potentials for long after that.

The second project was process improvement. Comcast used Richard Chang's *Ten Tools for Quality* with much success. You can use any problem solving model you want. In our project, the Comcast high potential leaders had to read his book and also collect employee retention data to use in an exercise in the class. Once leaders knew about influence and perspective, they needed to know how to move the needle on a key metric. It does not matter what the metric is, leaders need to know how to move their businesses forward. Self-aware leaders know how to do this faster: through others. They must understand how to take a group through a problem solving process. Leadership and facilitation are two different things. Key learning is allowing others to have input and ideas on how to make the upgrade.

The two samples on the following pages detail the assignment as presented to the Comcast leaders.

Sample 1: Community Investment Action Learning Assignment

Introduction:

You now understand the power of promoting corporate citizenship by way of our visit to Children's Hospital of Philadelphia (CHOP). Now the opportunity is yours to apply what you learned in your market; to implement based on the premise that in order to be a great corporate leader you must also be a great civic leader.

Assignment:

Use the following guidelines (that mirror our Development Dimensions International (DDI) training on influential leadership) to complete your community investment assignment.

STRATEGY

- Connect with your local contact for community investment to understand the steps involved in scoping a project.

- Identify key internal and external stakeholders and define what strategies you will use to sell this initiative with management and employees.

- Sequence each of the strategies in a manner that will set the business, others, and yourself up for success.

PACKAGING

- Anticipate what type of reactions you might expect from each of your stakeholder groups.

- Brainstorm methods to increase involvement. Goal is at least 25 people per project.

COMMITMENT

- Recruit a team of Comcast volunteers to support this initiative. The majority of this group should be outside of your direct reports and must include at least two other functions.

- Communicate how the exercise links to our community investment strategy.

- Successfully complete the activity.

- Identify what a long term commitment to this organization looks like for you/Comcast.

Criteria for Success:

- At least three different functions are represented in your team.

- Must include management and frontline employees.

- Minimum of 25 participants per project.

- FOL participants may not fundraise/"touch" dollars.

- Stay aligned and connected with your divisional community investment contact.

Deliverables:

The assignment requires that you produce an executive summary with the following items.

- An objective statement that summarizes the initiative and impact in one sentence.

- A list of a cross-functional project team and Comcast volunteers that drove your success.

- Bulleted action statements that summarize steps taken to achieve success.

- A bulleted list of 3-5 lessons learned that speak to how what you did will influence your behaviors as a leader in your real job.

Sample reports will be provided to all (via SharePoint site) as a model for best practices. Individual feedback will be provided in a written format to each participant at the June session. Feedback will be based on items listed above as well as how successful participants are in demonstrating the FOL program's core competencies. Participants may also submit drafts of their report prior to the deadline in order to receive feedback.

Due Dates:

April 3rd—A one-page divisional *status* report in the provided template to be distributed to [names], your manager, your local public affairs contacts, and your divisional cohort coach via email in a Word attachment. You should have buy-in from your local, regional, and divisional community investment leader prior to sending this email.

May 8th—A divisional *final* report in the provided template to be distributed to [names], your manager, your divisional cohort coach, and your divisional community investment leader via email in a Word attachment. This will entail a one-page executive summary for each person in your divisional cohort.

Sample 2: Process Improvement Action Learning Project

Introduction:

Just like with your community investment project, this goal in this exercise is to apply what you learned to a live business challenge. The application will begin with a project but should address a process upgrade in the end.

Assignment:

Tackle a real workplace problem that is linked to key operational initiatives (macro to micro) using a structured approach to solving the problem. Work with your manager/coach as well as your divisional FOL teammates for additional resources/help where needed. Use these guidelines for your problem solving project:

- Apply all six steps of the problem solving model.

- Follow the rules of brainstorming during all brainstorming sessions.

- Use the most appropriate voting method(s).

- Develop, use, and analyze at least four tools of quality (any from Dr. Chang's book).

Timeline:

Date	Deliverable	Distribution
June 19	Draft of individual PS/DO due (Will be presented to HQ operations leaders for feedback on 6/22)	One document per divisional team. Send to: cohort team; cohort coach; managers of participants; FOLA in your division
June 24	Individual feedback received on PS/DO	N/A
August 7	Submit individual status report	One document per individual participant. Send to: cohort team; cohort coach; manager of participant
July–September	Divisional webinars (3): Attend monthly con calls and invite market leaders to profile best practices as needed	N/A
October 2	Final divisional executive summaries due	Same as June 19 plus related divisional and HQ operations leaders
October 13–14	Group discussion regarding executive summaries	N/A

Report Format:

Ask your FOL Alumni participant sponsor for samples of what they produced and the template will be available on the SharePoint site. Final individual status reports may not exceed four pages. Final divisional executive summaries include a one-page executive summary for the division and one page that summarizes each individual project.

All individual reports must include:

- Your problem statement, desired outcome, and actual results.
- How you analyzed potential causes, and the true root causes of the problem in rank order with the most likely cause as #1.
- Your top five possible solutions.
- Your best solution(s) and why (using pros/cons).
- Your completed action plan.
- How you will/have evaluated progress from the implementation of the solution(s).
- Leadership lessons learned.

Use nontraditional approaches to make your key points through someone else's voice. You've carefully identified three to five key behaviors you are targeting in the program you have designed. You know that if you want people to really grasp and embrace the new way of leading, you're going to want to make the point a few different ways. You, as the trainer, cannot be the sole source of inspiration. You can't be the only one paving a new path of leadership for your participants. The design must incorporate training professionals, non-training experts from your organization, and outside experts. The points can be made literally or metaphorically, but the repetition will drive stronger adoption. Remember that everyone learns differently. At Comcast, we used operational leaders to translate major project case studies to learn from. We also used community leaders, who had nothing to do with cable or Internet, but who had a key message. For example, we used Jane Golden from the Philadelphia Mural Arts program and how she shared the paintbrush. Sometimes, you could use either the *Harvard Business Review* or a kids' story like *The Little Prince* to make the same exact point. Lastly, use alumni of the program to be peer mentors. They've been there, done that. They know how the program is designed. They also never let the current participants off easy. They will let them trip, but they won't let them fall. It's one of our most successful aspects of the program, and it's another way for alumni to receive positive reinforcement for their new way of leading.

Learning outside the classroom can prove to be more valuable than training inside the classroom. If you talk to people who work in student life on a college campus, many believe you learn as much outside the classroom as you do inside. The same holds true with this type of leadership program. As a training professional facilitating leadership development, building "touch points" into the instructional design is critical to assessing learner progress. Six days of phenomenal training won't always do the trick. Yes, you will always have eager learners that will want to connect with you outside the classroom for some practical advice, but as a designer you'll need to find a way to pull it out of more than just a few. As leaders complete milestones during their action learning projects, they are asked to submit updates using standard templates. The templates come right from key principles used in the training as well as the three to five key focal points of the program. Reviewing and providing the individual feedback is one of the most time-consuming aspects of administering this program, but it's also one of the most valuable. Whether it is feedback via track changes on a Word document or via a video call, this individual attention is critical to full adoption of the model. Below are templates for individual submissions.

Sample 1: Community Investment Project Summary Template

<u>Objective:</u> Create a one-sentence statement that identifies the link of goal, purpose, and overall business.

<u>Organization:</u> List the organization you are working with (name, location, and contact person).

<u>Comcast Stakeholders:</u> List the individuals in HR, Community Affairs, Government Affairs, and anyone else you have consulted with on this project.

<u>Project Team:</u> List the names of those individuals who contributed to making this initiative a success (including the volunteers).

<u>Leadership Takeaways:</u> List three things you learned about the "how" of this process. Be specific in identifying behaviors here.

As you type in these items, ask if you are saving the world (macro) or feeding a family (micro).

Strategy	Packaging	Commitment
1.	1.	1.
2.	2.	2.
3.	3	3.
4.	4.	4.
5.	5.	5.

Sample 2: Process Improvement Project Summary Template

Name, Title, Team
Location/Business Unit
Project Background
Two to three sentences explaining project background/context. **Team Participants** List of team participants and their functional areas of responsibility.

Problem Statement (PS)	Desired Outcome (DO)
One sentence PS.	One sentence DO.

Status as of September 28, 2011	Next Steps
• **Actual Result: In bold. One sentence that responds to DO.** • **Financial Impact: If possible, calculate the estimated/actual financial impact.** • Two to three other bullets.	• Three to five next steps.

Leadership Lessons Learned
Three bullets on what you learned as a leader and how it helps you in your real job.

NOTE: Keep this entire report under one page and feel free to submit in advance for feedback.

Build catchphrases that make your key teachings conversational. Bumper stickers. They are to the point. They are catchy and memorable. As you build your program, you will find yourself clinging to its 3–5 central behaviors—bumper sticker style catchphrases. Maybe they have been initiated by your learners in the heat of the lesson. Maybe they were intentionally and carefully scripted by you or your team. But, wow! They help. As you reflect on the content of this book you may be able to think of some of them. Here's the deal. One size does not fit all in terms of bumper stickers. They need to happen differently for each program. But, make no mistake, they need to happen. If I asked an alumnus of one of my programs about "the three elements of the vendor-led model" we taught them, or if I asked for the definition of a key leadership term from an executive who spoke to them, they would smile politely and, at best, venture a guess at remembering. They simply wouldn't remember. But if I asked them why they are control freaks, or about the feed a family versus solve world hunger tactic, or about how they were able to connect the dots last week—well, they'd likely still be talking. These catchphrases are hooks and these hooks become permanent fixtures in driving the leader's self-awareness.

Embrace the fact that business literacy is leadership development. There is an extreme difference between coaching and profitable coaching. It's no different than the difference between growth and profitable growth. One is simply more, the other is magnificent. Learning the key elements of a coaching conversation is generally simple. Define the difference between a result and a behavior, clarify how to position the conversation so the coachee owns it, and be a good listener through the process. You can use a five-step model and rectangle model or no model at all. What makes the difference between good and great coaches is that they know what drives the business and how their employees contribute. If they look at a weekly or monthly report that shows numerous productivity metrics, how do they know which one they should coach about?

- Is coaching supposed to fit all the metrics that are below the goal? No, because employees generally cannot digest a coaching conversation around four or five areas of improvement at once. There needs to be focused attention on improving specific areas.

- Is it coaching to fit the one that's most below goal? Not necessarily. While you want all your employees to be at or above expectations for all their goals, you need to first look at what's going on in the business. Which is more valuable: a 10 percent increase in productivity around their best metric or their worst?

Self-aware leaders know their people and their business. They make decisions every day on what and how to prioritize. If their business is evolving, leaders need to be taught how the definition of success has been altered. As the definition of insanity states, you cannot expect to do the same thing and get different results.

Closing Thoughts

Designing, managing, and facilitating this type of program can be both professionally and personally fulfilling. Why? First, it will build your credibility within your organization as adding value. Action learning projects draw attention to people and when those people complete the project, you will be the catalyst they remember. These types of programs will build you a strong network. You will quickly have trusted allies in every arm of the business. Allies you can call on in times of need. Finally, this type of program changes people's lives. It's powerful, and you must respect that. The relationships you build with a handful of participants will not only shape their lives for the better but also yours.

References

Bienhocker, E., I. Davis, and L. Mendonca. (2009). Trust in Business is Running Out. *Harvard Business Review* 54 (6): 1–8.

Birkinshaw, J., and C. Gibson. (2004). Building Ambidexterity into Organizations. *MIT Sloan Management Review* 45 (4): 47–55.

The Catholic Education Resource. (2011). St. Ignatius. http://www .catholiceducation.org

Gladwell, Malcolm. (2011). *Outliers: The Story of Success.* New York: Back Bay Books.

Glassdoor: An Inside Look at Jobs and Companies. (2011). Gibson Guitar Reviews. http://www.glassdoor.com/Reviews/Gibson-Guitar-Reviews-E6869.htm.

Healy, Riat. (2007). "The ATM in the Church Lobby." *TIME.* http:// www.time.com/time/business/article/0,8599,1648022,00.html

Hill, Napoleon. (2008). *The Law of Success: The Master Wealth-Builder's Complete and Original Lesson Plan for Achieving Your Dreams.* New York: Tarcher.

Ibarra, Herminia. (2004). *Working Identity: Unconventional Strategies for Reinventing Your Career.* Boston: Harvard Business Press.

Keidel, Robert. (1995). *Seeing Organizational Patterns: A New Theory and Language of Organizational Design.* San Francisco: Berrett-Koehler Publishers.

Keidel, Robert. (2010). *The Geometry of Strategy: Concepts for Strategic Management.* New York: Routledge.

Krakauer, Jon. (1996). *Into the Wild.* New York: Anchor Books.

Laipple, Joseph S. (2006). *Precision Selling: A Guide for Coaching Sales Professionals.* Atlanta: Performance Management Publications.

Melville, Kevin. (2006). *The School Dropout Crisis: Why One-Third of All High School Students Don't Graduate and What Your Community Can Do About It.* Richmond, VA: The University of Richmond Pew Partnership for Civic Change.

Rowley, Ian. (2009). Introducing the Nissan Leaf Electric Vehicle. *Bloomberg Businessweek, The Auto Beat.* http://www.businessweek.com/autos/autobeat/archives/2009/08/post_4.html

Starbucks Investor Relations. (2010). FY2010 Annual Report. http://phx.corporateir.net/External.File?item=UGFyZW50SUQ9NzkkzODl8Q2hpbGRJRD0tMXxUeXBlPTM=&t=1

Toogood, Granville N. (1996). *The Articulate Executive: Learn to Look, Act and Sound Like a Leader.* New York: McGraw-Hill.

Watkins, Michael. (2003). *The First 90 Days: Critical Success Strategies for New Leaders at All Levels.* Boston: Harvard Business Press.

Wharton University of Pennsylvania, Knowledge @ Wharton. (2009). "A World Transformed: What Are the Top 30 Innovations of the Last 30 Years?" http://knowledge.wharton.upenn.edu/article.cfm?articleid=2163

Index

ABOUT THE AUTHORS

Daniel P. Gallagher

Dan Gallagher has over 15 years of experience in leadership and organizational development roles with organizations such as Comcast, Commerce Bank, Hay Group, Cahners Publishing, and Saint Joseph's University. Since 2000, Dan has worked at Comcast and is now the vice president of learning and development. In this role he is responsible for the training strategy and resource optimization for 20,000 employees in Comcast's business units.

Dan attended Saint Joseph's University, where he graduated cum laude with a bachelor's degree in sociology, served as the Hawk mascot, and completed a master's degree in training and organizational development.

Dan served on the Philadelphia Society for Human Resource Management (PSHRM) board for nine years, where his tenure as chapter president (2007 2008) brought record-setting growth and contributed to him receiving the 2008 Delaware Valley HR Person of the Year award. Dan was a regional finalist for the 2009 2010 White House Fellowship program. Dan currently serves on City Year's Human Potential Advisory Board.

He was an adjunct instructor at Temple University and Saint Joseph's University and guest lectured at the University of Pennsylvania. Dan has spoken at numerous international conferences, including the Society for Human Resource Management, the North American Balanced Scorecard, and the American Society for Training and Development.

In 2006, Dan co-founded Generous Generations, a community organization that promotes generosity by connecting families with service opportunities. Dan is a 2008 Leadership Philadelphia Fellow and serves on their board. In 2010 he founded Gallagher Leadership, LLC.

As a member of the Saint Joseph's University National Alumni Board, Dan initiated the first ever National Day of Service (2008). Today, it is Global Community Day and attracts 1,000 volunteers annually. In 2010, Saint Joseph's University presented Dan with the Ignatius Award for his ongoing commitment to service.

He has twice successfully completed the marine corps marathon in Washington, D.C. Dan lives in suburban Philadelphia with his wife and four sons.

www.gallagherleadership.com
dan@gallagherleadership.com

Joseph Costal

Joe Costal teaches writing, public speaking, and leadership development at Richard Stockton College and Saint Joseph's University. He also teaches English at Oakcrest High School in Mays Landing, New Jersey, where he was named "Teacher of the Year" in 2010. Joe graduated from Rowan University with a master's degree in public relations and a bachelor's degree in English. He also served on the university's board of trustees. Over the past 10 years, Joe has been heavily involved in student leadership and has advised numerous student advocacy organizations on various campuses. He contributes his writing to Constitution Daily, the official blog of the National Constitution Center, and edits his own blogs on writing and film. Joe's writing has received accolades from the Columbia Scholastic Press Association and the Garden State Press Association. He lives "down the shore" in Cape May County, New Jersey, with his wife and four children.